HIJACKED

HIJACKED

Our REPUBLIC, Unless We Can SAVE IT

Peter H. Calfee &
J. Kevin Dolan

POLINOMICS™
PRESS

Hijacked: Our Republic, Unless We Can Save It

Copyright © 2025 Peter H. Calfee and J. Kevin Dolan

No part of this book may be reproduced or transmitted in any form or by any means, electronic or mechanical, including photocopying and recording, or by any information storage or retrieval system, except as may be expressly permitted by the 1976 Copyright Act or in writing from the publisher. Requests for permission should be addressed to authors@polinomicspress.com.

Published by Polinomics™ Press

979-8-9986192-0-5 - Paperback
979-8-9986192-1-2 - Hardcover
979-8-9986192-2-9 - eBook

Contents

Dedication vii

Introduction...1

Chapter 1: Critical Thinking.....................................13

Chapter 2: Education..33

Chapter 3: Religion, Faith, And Values....................45

Chapter 4: History..61

Chapter 5: Political Systems....................................71

Chapter 6: Economic Systems..................................91

Concluding Thoughts 103

Appendices...111

    Appendix 1a: Critical Terms and Concepts to Be Applied in Critical Thinking 112

    Appendix 1b: "An Obituary for Common Sense" 123

    Appendix 1c: "The Unsinkable Ship *Titanic America*"... 126

    Appendix 1d: Javier Milei's Speech to the World Economic Forum (WEF) January 17, 2024 130

    Appendix 1e: Colorado Past Governor Richard Lamm on the Ease of Destroying America.. 146

    Appendix 1f: Thought-Provoking Quotations from Thomas Sowell and Many Others 149

Appendix 2a: Education—Internal Public School
Competition Mechanics 178

Appendix 5a: Tucker Carlson and Bret Weinstein
Discuss the World Health Organization's Attempt to
Reduce American Sovereignty 181

Appendix 5b: Voting and Individual Responsibilities 186

Appendix 5c: Javier Milei's Speech to the United Nations
on September 24, 2024 188

Appendix 5D: Podcast Recommendations..................................... 198

Appendix 6a: Measuring Vision—True North, Quantum Leap
Logic, and Reverse Analysis 199

Appendix 6b: Successor Planning 203

Appendix 6c: Cycle of Freedom... 207

Acknowledgments 213
About the Authors 215
Index 219

DEDICATION

I want to dedicate this book to those critical thinkers with common sense, who have, for as long as we can remember, thought that something was wrong in our pursuit of the American Ideal . . . that but for some change in governance, approach, and non-situational application, we were and are at risk of losing it all!

As a student of history, evidence of a partial or total lack of common sense and critical thinking throughout the decades and centuries led us to review tumultuous times starting from before the Revolutionary War. Topics and themes were and are often similar to what we confront today. A reading of "Common Sense," an anonymous compilation of essays from Thomas Paine, provided a template for what we believed could be a similar exposition today of eternal truths and the application of them to our daily lives. This led to examination of topics like Education, Religion/Faith/Values, History, Politics, and Economics, which are woven like threads in a tapestry and a visual representation of progress of humankind throughout the millennia. We remain determined to uncover what went wrong over time within the study of topics mentioned, what was needed to understand why, and to incorporate tools and techniques to correct the "wrong" and identify the "right" path for humankind and our collective future.

With the help of books like this, we may still be able to right the ship and truly answer in the affirmative that we have indeed defended and preserved our constitutional republic in all its glory.

Peter H. Calfee

This book has been an endeavor to give back. The commercial success is unknown and not important. Bringing this book to life is our effort to pay forward the gifts we have received from others who have influenced our lives and helped us become modestly successful. This book is written in appreciation of all those who have set the precedent for me—those not looking for repayment, but rather, seeking to inspire their friends and coworkers as well as contribute to society's development. They are my Critical Thinkers: Colonel Bob Nugent, Trevor Gamble (naval carrier pilot and Dean of Students Denison University), Bill Henderson Ph.D., Captain Ed Brown, Captain Ron Moran, Captain Bill Jenney, Major General Archer Durham, Captain Rich O'Such, Jerry Rosenbloom Ph.D., Captain Carl Price, Captain Terry Jackson, Captain Tony DeSantis, Bill Hubble, Ron Simmons, Joe Russo, Jim Cuminale, Gordon Cooper, Matt Barry, Adrian Teel and Rahul Srivastava. These are just a few of the individuals who contributed to my life and development. I will be forever grateful for your impact and that of many others, too numerous to mention.

Finally, I would like to dedicate this book to my grandchildren (Marlou, Grier, Stoneham, and Gardner). They and their generation are the seed corn of our future. We hope this book may assist our great country in getting back on the right track, preparing that generation and successive ones for a bright future. We hope and pray that their generation and future generations may be as fortunate as our generation in experiencing the wonderful and challenging freedoms that we have.

J. Kevin Dolan

INTRODUCTION

The human development journey has never been easy. The mission to improve the daily lives of billions of people has been marked by struggles, trials, and errors. At times, that progress has been halted, detoured, and even hijacked. Yet still we seek to keep moving forward.

The goal of this book is to help us continue our journey toward this greater good with a deep understanding of both our successes and our failures. The progress of mankind, a better life for more people, and the protection of individual rights all result from an emphasis on increasing the greater good of all humanity. By absorbing the lessons of the past and keeping our focus on the greater good, we can avoid the worst mistakes in the present and embrace the prospect of a brighter future for the United States of America.

Even as our Founding Fathers managed to get everyone on board to ratify our nation's founding documents, they were aware that a certain flexibility was needed to accommodate the ways our country would change over time. While the Declaration of Independence and the Constitution are amazingly perceptive documents, they required compromises to gain agreement.

The Declaration of Independence conveyed a signature vision based on natural laws, while the Constitution creatively compromised certain Values in order to give birth to our nation. They were limited in scope and didn't address every potential issue the country might face—but they didn't need to. The genius of these documents was that, rather than always immediately and directly addressing issues, they guided our society to continually improve in our brief time on this earth.

We may find it easy to make observations about what is right or wrong with the human condition, families, Education, health, the economy, and our Political System at any given moment, but much is lost as time passes and conversations continue to unfold. It is only when we take the time to reflect upon our personal goals, the various achievements of our society, our present, and our future that we can see the bigger picture and intentionally nudge society forward. To begin to know what is right and what is wrong in this bigger picture, we must start by Thinking Critically.

This book reflects upon the tools that have guided us to where we are today and uses those tools to assemble a complete picture of the focus needed for mankind to continue making effective progress. Thus, we will discuss the fundamental tools of any lasting society: Critical Thinking; Education; Religion, Faith, and Values; History; Political Systems; and Economic Systems. Taken together, these tools and systems define the fabric of our society.

Throughout history, many of the great models of humankind's progress have eroded and eventually crumbled. The Greeks, the Romans, the empires of Portugal and Spain, the Dutch trading empire, the hegemony of France in the seventeenth century, and the expansive and once-dominating British Empire—all of them eventually lost their momentum and slowed to a stop. Some had midlife crises, like Rome, and became something new altogether. But what resulted was never the same or better, often only serving to slow the fall. Each of these civilizations either forgot or compromised the tools and Values that once made it great, leading to its ultimate downfall.

Before their demise, there was a time when each of these civilizations was being developed, sustained, and improved over time. Yet the educational system we have today has failed to reinforce—let alone pass on—the value systems, historical figures, and cultural icons that were critical to these civilizations' rise.

Without Critical Thinking; a sound application of Education, Values, and Faith; and observations of History, civilizations cannot evaluate and lay out a path for continued progress. Societies need to reflect eternal truths; without them, they go awry with time. There is never an easy path to success. It is only by growing our understanding of these bedrock systems of society and their ideological underpinnings that we can hope to continue in our march toward progress.

Thousands of societies have failed to do so and have fallen into prisons of their own design as a result. Communism, fascism, and pure socialism are all examples of this. Though they go by different names, they are all single-party political structures that produce the same result: declining societies due to excessive control by the state.

Each of these paths results in the consolidation of power into a single party designed to benefit those holding the reins. The language adopted by these regimes is intended to endear them to the citizenry while bringing them under total control of the party. Once the citizenry loses its ability to demonstrate or revolt, the party frequently evolves into a one-person dictatorship with absolute power. Think of Stalin in Russia, Mao in China, Peron in Argentina, Castro in Cuba, Pol Pot in Cambodia, the Ayatollah in Iran, Ortega in Nicaragua, or Chavez and Maduro in Venezuela. Finally, when the leader in power dies, so too does the regime. Like clockwork, each one ends in failure.

The United States, as a beacon for the rest of the world, has arrived at a crossroads. There are hard choices to be made, but there is also hope. We can choose to forge a positive path forward—all while acknowledging, combating, defusing, and defeating the violent and evil forces that would like to see us abandon the time-tested eternal truths, move toward authoritarianism, and eventually fall into major decline.

But how do we forge such a path? What role is there for those who seek to avoid conflict, contention, and strife? How do we reconcile our desire for mutually determined progress, friendship, respect, and simple kindness? What is necessary for the pursuit of optimism, collegiality, and teamwork that historically would define a functioning political structure? How do we avoid defaulting to an attitude of "might makes right" as the arbiter of our actions and discussions?

And why have we lost our way in the first place? Could it be that we . . .

1. Have looked outside ourselves for guidance and hope that may not exist?

2. Have ignored the need for sustainable positive progress and replaced it with short-term fungible gains?

3. Have abandoned the basic human principles of goodness, righteousness, justice, fairness, responsibility, and accountability in favor of unyielding self-absorption, impatience, greed, and self-interest at the expense of others?

4. Have placed the individual above other societal concerns? Just as gasoline is not more important than the car, since neither works without the other, so too do the interests of the individual and those of society rest on one another. If we were to consider the

true meaning of *E Pluribus Unum* (out of many, one), we may find that teamwork, alliance, and goals achieved with mutual interests may present a path toward protecting the interests of the individual.

5. Have allowed others to attempt to direct and control us in a pursuit of power with little regard for our inalienable rights?

6. Have allowed others to usurp our thoughts, strategies, and inquiries and to take away responsibility for our actions? Put another way, have we given away the keys that drive our destiny?

We need to visualize a model of society that has a more singular purpose: to make it possible for all citizens to achieve what they are motivated to accomplish while also contributing to the greater good of humankind.

The human condition could be viewed as a drama of triumphs and failures, yet we continue to evolve. Observed over millennia, there is a consistency to human nature eventually getting it right. How do we do it? The fabric of our society and its social cohesion ebbs and flows. It is ever in flux. Yet through a constancy of purpose and attention to doing the right thing, we bring about progress and a slow forward movement of society. The result? We strengthen our connection with all that is right and just over time.

Often, the difference between success and failure comes down to a single question: Are we as a people pursuing numerous different goals or a singular, shared goal?

Pursuing a singular, shared goal is an incredibly large aim, which is why most people give up on pursuing it altogether. But to paraphrase baseball coaching legend John Scolinos, you don't change the size of the home plate to make things easier on a bad pitcher.

For over half a century, our culture has expanded the size of home plate and has shrunken the skill required to be a pitcher. The problem growing within our homes, within our marriages, in our parentage, and in our kids' discipline is just that: We have gotten away from teaching accountability. There is no consequence for failing to meet standards. Instead, we simply widen the plate.

The results are clear and devastating. The quality of Education is going downhill fast. Teachers have been stripped of the tools they need to educate and discipline our young people. If we are to grow again, we must hold ourselves to a higher standard—a standard of what we know to be right.

The glue that holds the fabric of society together is Critical Thinking. Critical Thinking is the process of questioning everything. Humankind has become so narrow in thought that even our alleged intellectuals of the day seem to have lost the ability to think about societal issues in a connected, comprehensive, or critical way.

Critical Thinking has long been the key to developing and ascending societies from the dregs of decay and ruin. It provides the building blocks for humanity to discover basic truths through inquiry and experience, trial and error, failure and accomplishment, and now through the use of artificial intelligence.

Without the ability to Think Critically, the progress and development of society is impossible. Without Critical Thinking, one merely stumbles through life, from one concept or idea to another, without taking time to analyze and address what is right and what might be wrong, misguided, deceptive, or harmful. Without the ability to think things through, make inquiries, and evaluate experience to guide a course of action, how does one know in which direction to go?

We make observations about our lives, family, Education, spiritual matters, economic actions, politics, health, technology, society, and more. The sum of all these observations locally, regionally, and nationally represents the societal fabric—the concept of community or national identity layered and built up over the millennia. These observations are our anchors—our means of starting from one point and continuing to another point with some sense that we are accomplishing something.

Despite the mistakes, missteps, and delays that inevitably occur, the growth of humankind is a clear imperative. While growth can sometimes happen by chance, it more often comes as the result of planning and goal-setting so that our achievements align with our desired goals. Goals are the things we establish to provide ourselves and others with a perspective of our achievement in the world. As such, our goals need to be crafted in such a way that we can clearly measure our direction, effort, movement, accomplishment, and growth.

Direction and intentional growth depend on our ability to Think Critically, but there's more to the puzzle. How do we know what is true and what is a fabrication or disinformation? And where do we get the information to know what to accept, believe, honor, or acknowledge as a rule or law to guide our observations? How do we know if what we see makes sense or is total nonsense?

The information we need comes from our Education and ability to assemble knowledge of humankind's History. One might say that History was created through the past application of Critical Thinking, Education, Faith, and Values. The assembly and development of these building blocks are vital. We don't want to be guided simply by opinions but instead by the empirical reality of what has worked in the past, what continues to work, and what could work forever without compromise.

All aspects of life are related. All human endeavors have a purpose—some good and some bad—but a purpose nonetheless. One's purpose can be to exist; to survive; to procreate; to protect family and friends; or to guard one's village, town, city, nation, climate, or even the universe. There are as many purposes in life as there are people. So how do we begin to understand our purpose as a nation and as individuals?

History teaches us what humans have done right and wrong in the past. It also shows how people throughout time have posed the question of the meaning of their existence, and it serves as a witness to the growth of humanity as a gathering of people from family and communal gatherings into villages, urban areas, and nation-states that require Political and Economic Systems. By combining History with the building blocks of Education, we can examine where we have been, where we are now, and where we want to go.

The examples of our founders and other historical figures can help inform our direction. These models do not represent perfect people but rather people who lived at a point in human History from whom we can learn. By reflecting on their choices and experiences, we can benefit from the stories of people who were both successful and flawed.

Given the time and place they lived in, can't we appreciate their contributions to human progress while also recognizing the limitations of their time? Are we not better informed and thus more capable of applying their lessons without also repeating their mistakes? Shouldn't we be able to critically analyze their History, differentiating the good causes from the bad? If we hope to learn from our History, such analysis must be the foundation for improving the fabric of society we seek to preserve.

Do we really expect society to have been perfect from the beginning? Or does it make more sense that our ideas have progressed and will continue to progress toward more rational behavior over time? When we seek to erase and tear down all memories of how things were done incorrectly in the past, we lose the historical data that could help us avoid repeating the same mistakes in the future.

There is a certain consistency to human nature, but we do not remain static. The fabric of our society is either strengthening or weakening, but one thing is sure: It will not remain the same. Thus, we should each strive to contribute to the positive evolution of humankind's development.

To understand where society is going next, we must apply Critical Thinking to connect the dots between important issues and to help us understand the big picture. To do so, it may be helpful to look through the prism of our responsibility to future generations.

Are we preparing future generations properly?

To answer that question, we must define what proper preparation looks like. Who decides what it is? And what Political and Economic Systems will shape and define them?

What is needed most is a clear vision of the ingredients needed to help humankind achieve its optimal state. Nothing stands alone. Whether rightly or wrongly, humankind moves forward together. We strive despite ourselves, eventually producing long-term progress. But we often lose our way through missteps and failures. How does humankind survive despite these failures? And how do we avoid repeating patterns of self-destruction that stem from structural flaws in our human condition?

To move forward together, we must avoid compromising eternal truths. These truths are the universally accepted highest standards of behavior and belief that society has evolved to recognize over time. But to ever begin to analyze and discuss them, we must begin with Critical Thinking.

Once again, we come to the conclusion that the United States—like much of the world—is at a crossroads where hard choices must be effectively made and communicated by its citizenry. In the pages to follow, we will present a positive path forward while acknowledging and presenting some of the evil forces that attempt to take us down the low road.

The chapters of this book will lay out the concepts that define the solution with honesty, fact, sanity, and clear-headedness, considering each of the fundamental elements necessary for successful societies:

1. **Critical Thinking**

2. **Education** and its use

3. **Religion, Faith, and Values** and their constant importance in the pursuit of eternal truth

4. **History**, which allows us to know the past and improve upon it

5. **Political Systems** and their influence, both good and bad

6. **Economic Systems** and their influence, both good and bad

As we move forward, let us rely upon sage advice from C. S. Lewis in *Mere Christianity*: "If you look for truth, you may find comfort in the end; if you look for comfort, you will not get comfort or truth—only soft soap and wishful thinking to begin, and in the end, despair."

So let's begin our search for vision by taking the high road and committing to look for truth. The road may be difficult, but it is well worth the journey!

Suggested Reading Method:

The following chapters are short, but they ask a lot of questions and give a lot of information for your consideration. Therefore, we suggest one of two methods for reading this book.

1. Read a chapter a day, and let the thoughts sit with you for a while. Then, after completing the chapters, each day, skim each of the chapters again then go to the appendices mentioned in the chapter, if there are any, and read them for their impact on the chapter itself.

2. Read a chapter each day and also any appendices referred to in the chapter or numbered to demonstrate that it strongly relates to the chapter. And let those thoughts gestate with you.

CHAPTER 1
CRITICAL THINKING

As we see in the application of scientific thought, one often cannot prove that something is verifiably correct; instead, the most one can do is demonstrate that something is not incorrect at present.

But this path is not an easy one to walk. Everyone wants to have their thoughts validated. We all harbor a certain confirmation bias. Even when the veracity of our thoughts is subject to debate, we still want others to agree with us to make us feel more reasonable. But by seeking only confirmation, we put ourselves in a dangerous position by blinding ourselves to what is actually true. The solution to this trap is in our thinking—*Critical Thinking*.

Critical Thinking is the process of questioning everything. It is a foundational tool of reasoning that has been essential for the development of humankind for millennia.

Unfortunately, as a society, it is a skill we seem to have largely lost. Across multiple generations, we have seen a decline in our ability to question and apply Critical Thinking. These days, even our intellectuals seem to have lost the ability to think about societal issues comprehensively and critically.

If this skill is lost forever, our culture will never survive. It will continue in the same long, slow descent that crippled the great civilizations in History that have come before. Unless we relearn how to think critically, our society will be buried beside them in the annals of textbooks and documentaries.

To apply Critical Thinking regarding any issue, our analysis should begin with the same simple question: *What could be wrong with this proposed thought?*

For example, we regularly see media outlets across the political spectrum make claims that clearly favor their own point of view. We see these claims on television channels, on our phones, and in the headlines. Pundits on both sides of the aisle make bold claims about how an application of their policies would correct things, but their propositions seem too good to be true.

Often, it is just that. These ideologues point out massive problems and then propose quick fixes instead of realistic solutions. But a reasonable person knows from life experience that the person offering a Band-Aid usually doesn't stick around long enough to find out if you need surgery.

Another case study in Critical Thinking considers the phrase, "Follow the science." In times past, this used to mean applying Critical Thinking and drawing your own conclusions based on the data. But in recent years, it has become a slogan for those who would rather not explain their methodologies whatsoever. "Follow the science" is now mostly an instruction for blind obedience.

However, with an awareness of History, logic, and the application of spiritual Values, one can draw independent conclusions as to the validity of proposed positions. When confronted with a perspective, it is helpful to pose a few questions to determine if what we are hearing or seeing is true. A good example is when someone claims the Declaration of Independence or something in our Constitution is obsolete.

These questions to ask may be as simple as the following:

1. How would our nation have become the most powerful country on the face of the earth without these two documents?

2. Was it not by virtue of our political and governing structure?

3. Who created that structure of government, and what was their reasoning?

Anyone who studies our Founding Fathers quickly becomes aware that the Founders applied a comprehensive understanding of History when they crafted our founding documents. They used Critical Thinking and evaluated what made the nations of the past successful—and what led to their downfall. Then they applied the principles that they knew worked. The results speak for themselves. Just look at what the United States has accomplished since its inception with the governmental structure and documents the Founding Fathers gave us.

Free thought is how we both form and disqualify perspectives. Through questioning and analysis, we weigh and understand the value found in dogma and tradition in our journey to understanding truth while seeking the empirical truth. Promoting Critical Thinking and encouraging open dialogue are essential for addressing societal issues and encouraging diverse perspectives. By listening to voices that disagree with our own, we prevent ourselves from becoming trapped by ideological conformity.

We are all familiar with the vast knowledge base existing today within the servers, databases, and internet clouds throughout the world. In the context of Critical Thinking, the problem is that the internet lacks wisdom. Especially with the rise of artificial intelligence and more efficient algorithms, the internet produces answers, but rarely are they tested for being prudent. It may appear that it is not wise to take the human mind out of the analysis.

Wisdom is only possible when thought is questioned in a way that applies knowledge, experience, good judgment, and Common Sense. Such thought presumes a considerable rationale has been developed with a logical string of ideas that drive toward a conclusion that directs the thinker towards a chosen goal, such as the advancement of humankind. This process presumes logic is vital to understanding and advancing the human condition.

Even before the hunter-gatherers, our ancestors were reactive and habitual. It was instinctive back then to advance the group toward the two basic goals of survival and procreation. Once we add the moral imperative of religious belief, we approach the world of eternal truths.

Over the course of human development, we eventually discovered that certain truths were inalienable. As Americans, these truths held our diverse peoples together when previously only a crown and scepter had been able to do so. Humankind had to turn to basic, common-sense principles and Critical Thinking to discover and apply what we perceived to be our inalienable rights.

FREEDOM TO THINK, QUESTION, AND SPEAK

A look at History should readily show the three essential characteristics assisting the creation of better societies: the Right to Think, Question, and Speak.

People have an innate desire to Question. From a young age, children ask questions to understand how they should respond to their parents and teachers. Although we continue to possess this natural curiosity, over time we often let shortcuts blind us to the natural simplicity of the process.

The inability to question limits public discourse. New, meaningful ideas do not have a fertile environment to grow and flourish. For Critical Thinking to become second nature in our social fabric, we must allow Thoughts and Speech to be open, free, and unconstrained. Without this allowance, the most important Thoughts of our most creative people may never see the light of day, thus hobbling progress.

When we promote the Freedom to Think, Question, and Speak, we reinforce the bedrock of all other freedoms. This allows us to grow individually while contributing to the freedom and progress of society.

APPLICATION OF COMMON SENSE

One of the easiest and first tools we as people develop and learn to apply is that of Common Sense. To utilize Common Sense, we must recognize what it is.

Webster's Dictionary states that *Common Sense* is "the ability to make sound judgments." Critical to that definition is the word *sound*. What may be sound to us could possibly not be sound to others. (See also appendix 1c.)

One could easily substitute that definition for the following litmus question: Can such proposed actions, policies, regulations, laws, or attributes lead to consistently correct outcomes that point humankind toward positive, sustainable progress? In other words, is the outcome well-constructed, consistent, and acceptable to not only you but the plurality of society?

Once the common-sense litmus test is passed, then a person may proceed to the next step, where the question of causal connection must be answered. Once a child learns that something may be a sound judgment, they naturally want to know what caused it.

Causality is "the relationship between cause and effect." *Logic* is a "system of reasoning," and thus, being logical is the process of "displaying consistency in reasoning." *Wisdom* is "understanding what is true, right, or lasting." Judgment is to Common Sense what erudition is to learning.

Even cases that make it all the way to the Supreme Court pivot on whether or not an action caused a result. That concept seems so simple, but this is a highly developed process. Thousands of years of human experience have evolved our understanding of what truly causes something else. By understanding this process, we can better predict outcomes and maximize the results.

In any discussion or debate, there are four concepts whose applications are paramount. It will be difficult for humankind to advance without the proper application of these cornerstone concepts.

1. Causality
2. Logic
3. Wisdom
4. Judgment

Finding the cause of *X* and then applying a logical development helps us understand how our present circumstances came to be. If we have identified a true problem (and not a symptom), then applying these four terms will help us identify a solution that can stand the test of time and strengthen our social fabric.

The word *premise* is important when determining where an idea came from. The beginning point of any discussion or argument in the classic sense is frequently referred to as the premise of the argument.

Webster defines *premise* as "a proposition on which an argument is based or from which a conclusion is drawn." The premise is the foundation of a logical set of statements to arrive at a sound conclusion. If one accepts the premise and the logic of the argument to follow, then one must accept the conclusion.

THE SOCIAL FABRIC OF SOCIETY

The social fabric is essential to maintaining a society. What is the social fabric? There may be numerous interpretations, but we propose it to be the material binding together all institutions and individuals within society. Yet this fabric is dynamic—it is constantly shifting, either weakening or strengthening.

Critical Thinking strengthens the fabric of society.

To understand this, we must first understand what our responsibilities are to society. An understanding of Rousseau's social contract helps here. We believe that an individual gives up their Darwinist (survival of the fittest or rule of physical power) capabilities in exchange for the benefit of society's protections under its laws and regulations. This exchange requires that the individual understands and agrees that one must follow the rules, laws, and mechanisms that exist to change what is faulty in society. This recognition of society's faults does not free us from personal responsibility—hence, the individual must remain accountable to their society.

A belief in oneself is vital to a belief in society. One must be and remain free to discover the boundaries of their own Thoughts. This does not mean that people should be encouraged to experiment with deviant behavior, but rather that they should be willing to broaden their horizons. Society must encourage such exploration. By doing such mental exploration, one is better able to Think Critically.

But when we lose that knowledge of self—as well as the responsibilities and accountability to Rousseau's social contract—we can be left with a road to chaos and destruction.

Frederic Bastiat, a French economist from the first half of the nineteenth century, made this insightful comment: "When plunder (and dispossession) becomes a way of life for a group of men in a society, over the course of time they create for themselves a legal system that authorizes it and a moral code that glorifies it," thus clearing the way for illegal and violent actions.

Likewise, Javier Millei, elected in November and installed in December of 2023 as president of Argentina, gave a powerful speech to the World Economic Forum on January 17, 2024, regarding the global attempt to hijack freedom. (See Appendix 1d for the entire speech.)

WHAT CONFLICTS WITH CRITICAL THINKING?

Before we continue, it is important to pause and discuss what happens when we fail to incorporate the previous building blocks in support of true Critical Thinking and the resulting strengthening of the fabric of society. Throughout History, some free societies have descended into indoctrination, while others have spiraled out of control by being overly open-minded.

These problems have been peculiarly consistent. Athens, the Roman Republic, Germany, and China are prime examples of civilizations destroying themselves via indoctrination. Meanwhile, both Robespierre's France and Lenin's Russia promoted far too many ideas at once and ended in mob rule and massacre. Both paths lacked Critical Thinking, but in different ways.

Indoctrination is "teaching to accept a system of thought uncritically." Information and logic are not to be questioned when being indoctrinated. With indoctrination, there is no learning to be applied. One is given information to spit back verbatim without question. Indoctrination is the twisted sibling of Education. It perverts thought and our understanding of the purpose of life. Critical Thinking is the opposite of indoctrination.

Any individual or institution that tries to indoctrinate people does not believe in the right of the individual to possess the Freedom to Think, Question, and Speak. (See also appendix 1e.)

As noted earlier, these freedoms are natural rights. That means that under natural law, as detailed throughout Roman History, the Renaissance, the Enlightenment, and even modern times, we rightfully possess these inalienable rights. If we are to maintain our freedoms, for which our Founding Fathers pledged their lives, fortunes, and sacred honor to each other, we must be dedicated to and make a commitment to protecting our right to Freedom of Thought, Questioning, and Speech. Unless we break the social contract, no one should be allowed to deprive us of these freedoms.

But when a person or persons intend to wrongfully deprive us of these freedoms, they threaten to hijack our freedoms. To hijack is to unlawfully seize a vehicle in transit and force it to go to a different destination or use it for one's own purposes. When forces attacking a society's expression of thoughts, beliefs, choices, and desires hijack the levers of a free-functioning society, the population may lose Faith in the entire system's integrity. A society cannot maintain and strengthen its fabric if its integrity is violated.

When people lack trust in their institutions, they inevitably begin to ask why they needed them to begin with. They rapidly decide that whatever exists must be the problem. They see loose threads in the fabric of society and begin to doubt the purpose of the entire fabric. Soon, every loose thread becomes a reason to burn the fabric. However, when people have a proper understanding and use Critical Thinking to accurately assess the problem and discern solutions, then the societal fabric can be repaired. But Critical Thinking without trust moves people to turn to fear and indoctrination as a safe harbor.

In addition to Freedom of Thought, Questioning, and Speech, a bedrock of the fabric of society is the integrity of the election process. Without confidence in our elections, the fabric of society can erode rapidly. Therefore, integrity and transparency in elections are imperative.

Note the result of Benito Mussolini's drive for power in 1922. He marched to Rome with his political supporters and militia and forced his appointment by Victor Emmanuel III, the last king of Italy. Mussolini used his Black Brigade and others to take advantage of a politically weak and divided government and to rule as the first fascist party in Europe. Mussolini became a model for Hitler and his Nazi Party's rise to power in 1933, being appointed chancellor by a weakened democracy that simply could no longer govern. Beware of the government that cannot govern.

Both historical movements—the rise of Mussolini and the rise of Hitler—effectively eliminated the last vestiges of democratic rule. They then imposed a totalitarian model onto those nations and immediately began indoctrinating children and adults to their whims. These governments allowed specific segments of a population to commit crimes, wreak havoc, and instill terror and fear in the lives and minds of the greater population. Because they needed people to trust that they had their best interests in mind, they shunned anyone who questioned the new ruling party.

As the citizenry acquiesced to these threats of force, they became complicit in the crimes of these regimes. Soon, a population such as that realizes the choices are simple: Compliance with nothing but active support for the regime or immediate removal from society. The result is annihilation and collapse.

Power-hungry politicians and factions often employ this technique. To shift from a democracy to a collectivist dictatorship, History has shown that regimes employ techniques like those espoused by community activist Saul Alinsky: "Accuse the other side of that which you are guilty." Using that technique, along with using words that sound good while doing the opposite, has worked to gain complete control. After all, in the words of Nazi Propaganda Minister Joseph Goebbels, "If you repeat a lie often enough, people will believe it, and you will even come to believe it yourself."

Similarly, the Bolsheviks in Russia took advantage of a corrupt and decaying monarchy. With the monarchy overthrown, the Russian people lay at the feet of a new dictatorship, one with neither the ability nor interest to apply the thesis of Karl Marx. Elites were arrested, the people's guns confiscated along with individual wealth, and a civil war erupted—which, ironically, evolved into the dictatorship of Stalin and the creation of a new elite, the communist party members. The revolution did not resolve any problems; it only changed the players. But by then no one was left to question it; the competition among the comrades in arms was murdered.

To understand the totalitarian structure, we need to look no further than the rise of communism from 1917 to date, the impact of the three Kim rulers in North Korea from 1949 to date, the Mullahs of Iran from 1979 to date, the totalitarian structure of chaos and decay in Russia under Vladimir Putin's rule from 1999 to date, and the terrorist philosophies of ISIS and Bin Laden/Al-Qaeda, among many other depraved rulers and regimes. (See chapter 5 for a fuller analysis of Political Systems.)

Such is the result when we fail to realize the importance of our societal fabric and when it is unwoven, piece by piece.

AVOIDING TOTALITARIANISM

It is helpful to identify what thought process might be employed to hijack Critical Thinking to eliminate freedom in order to create an elitist totalitarian structure. It is important to note that if those civilizations had exercised Critical Thinking, they could have avoided their fall into despotism and the elimination of freedom. But first comes anarchy.

We know what anarchy looks like. Saul Alinsky, a community organizer who attended the University of Chicago, promoted a model that clearly taught how to use anarchy to unravel a society. He was a longtime mentor and influencer of political leaders nationwide.

According to Alinsky, all that is necessary is to read and apply the rules from his book *Rules for Radicals (1971)*, including the following:

1. "Power is not only what you have, but what the enemy thinks you have."

2. "Whenever possible, go outside the expertise of the enemy."

3. "Ridicule is man's most potent weapon."

4. "Keep the pressure on. Never let up."

5. "If you push a negative hard enough, it will push through and become a positive."

6. "Pick the target, freeze it, personalize it, and polarize it."

It is unthinkable that the above rhetoric or Machiavellian thought, in general, has been a source of inspiration for our leadership over the prior decades. We need to think beyond our nation and culture to the influx of chaotic, divisive thoughts that have torn down our barriers to possessive, irrational, self-serving thought, which in turn threatens the very existence of our country and its institutions.

We see the lack of Critical Thinking over the decades reflected in public policies driven by progressive thought:

1. **Health-Care Policy.** Seize control of it with regulation. Hijack its operation. The imposition of laws and regulations can lead to "extra-national" rule through mechanisms that are designed to supersede national constitutions

2. **Poverty.** Institute procedures and programs that encourage government dependence. People are easier to control if the government provides everything for them to live.

3. **Welfare.** Take control of as many aspects of a person's life as possible: housing, income, cost of food, energy, transportation. People direct their calls for aid to the government.

4. **Debt.** Increase the national debt to an unsustainable level, and more poverty will be produced.

5. **Gun Policy.** Make inroads in the efforts to control the manufacturing of guns and ammunition while removing the ability of people to defend themselves. It is much easier to create a police state without interference from gun owners.

6. **Education.** Take control of what children learn in school.

7. **Religion.** Remove Faith from the classroom and government.

8. **Class Warfare.** Divide the population into as many diverse and separate groups as possible to emphasize differences, sow discord and disagreement, and establish socioeconomic discord.

TEN RULES FOR PROBLEM-SOLVING WITH CRITICAL THINKING

We have shown examples of leftist thought leaders who would destroy what our Founding Fathers and many patriots then and since then have created and maintained. Now we propose a list of ten rules that could be followed to more effectively and consistently apply Critical Thinking for the sustainability of our incredible Democratic Republic.

1. Understand that to Think, Question, and Speak are unalienable rights.

2. Make censorship a significant crime subject to legal penalties and possibly monetary awards.

3. Apply analytical skills.

4. Clearly identify the problem or issue.

5. Question whether that which is identified is a symptom or the actual problem or issue.

6. Once the true problem or issue has been identified with concurrence...

    a. Look for causality.

    b. Identify contributing actions, and

    c. State the negative effect or the positive potential of it.

7. Creatively offer several solutions.

8. Debate the pros and cons.

9. Ask litmus questions such as...

    a. Which of the potential solutions offers the preferred outcome consistent with the Values attributed to the fabric of society through the existing constitutional structure?

    b. Is the incentive and motivation system that would be put in place consistent with the Values of the current fabric of society, or does it even improve upon it?

    c. Would the solution, once put in place, be repetitive and sustainable for the long-term benefit of society?

10. Identify the individuals to be part of the team for the implementation of the solution, people who possess high character.

a. Participants need to be team players, understanding that their contribution to the team is a higher priority than personal gain.

b. Each individual must possess the skill required to effect their portion of the solution.

c. Look for participants who possess as many of the following characteristics as possible:

   i. Honesty

   ii. Integrity

   iii. Dependability

   iv. Consistency

   v. Persistence

   vi. Competitiveness

   vii. Open-mindedness

   viii. Creativity

   ix. Good communication

   x. Altruistic motives

   xi. Selflessness

   xii. Credibility

   xiii. Inspiration

As a further example, in the spring of 2005 (at an Overpopulation Conference in Washington, DC), Governor Richard Lamm of Colorado made the following points on how great nations commit suicide (by Mike Zeller posting on LinkedIn, August 21, 2016).

> If you believe that America is too smug, too self-satisfied, too rich, then let's destroy America. It is not that hard to do. No nation in history has survived the ravages of time. Arnold Toynbee observed that all great civilizations rise and fall and that "An autopsy of history would show that all great nations commit suicide." (See appendix 1e for more of his comments and complete speech.)

In short, Critical Thinking is presently in short supply. There appears to be an inability to understand the ramifications and consequences of a stated course of action. This lack of Critical Thinking is the first step in how a society such as ours can be hijacked.

To honor the sovereignty of our Constitution, its amendments, and the associated Bill of Rights, we look to Critical Thinking to provide the foundation for thought. We look to themes, concepts, and action steps to assist in the implementation and execution of Critical Thought.

One can now see the important sequence with our chapter ordering. Critical Thinking, as the first chapter, depends upon several important concepts that must be employed to avoid the hijacking of society. The application of Critical Thinking is enabled through Education but is informed by Religion, Faith, and the Values they create. Each chapter that follows is interdependent with every other chapter.

1. **Critical Thinking.**

2. **Education** and the imperative of an inquiring, rational population.

3. **Religion, Faith, and Values:** We express our faith in ideas, truths, and thoughts. What is necessary is Religion or some form of spirituality, which plays a role as an important source of Values, along with guidance from the family unit. The ability to push forward demands an awareness of what is fair, safe, useful, and right because our Values shape our laws.

4. **History:** A profound remembrance of what has gone before, of what was correct and progressive in the sense of advancement, and what led to conflict, war, and collapse—and the interwoven threads that have held and currently hold together the fabric of society. We cannot cherry-pick certain moments in History and erase others. History must be there in its entirety for all to see and for all to consider the lessons provided to all humankind.

5. **Political Systems:** The understanding of the pros and cons of all known systems.

6. **Economic Systems:** How we function collectively while acknowledging and protecting value for the individual.

As a wheel requires its spokes for structural integrity, so does the future of society depend on the concepts of these chapters as spokes for the wheel of humankind's advancement. Without Critical Thinking to guide us, the bicycle with broken spokes cannot be ridden, and we become lemmings blindly walking over the edge of the cliff. Society is complex. With Critical Thinking, we construct the foundations for all that follows in the advancement of humankind.

FREEDOM QUOTATIONS

True freedom consists of escaping the prison of prejudices and conventionalisms and forming our own opinions, even if they go against the grain.

(Mario Escobar, The Swiss Nurse, 2023)

Be a free thinker and don't accept everything you hear as truth. Be critical and evaluate what you believe in.

(Aristotle)

No problem can withstand the assault of sustained thinking.

(Voltaire)

Learn from yesterday, live for today, hope for tomorrow. The important thing is not to stop questioning.

(Albert Einstein)

Devotion to the truth is the hallmark of morality; there is no greater, nobler, more heroic form of devotion than the act of a man who assumes the responsibility of thinking.

(Ayn Rand)

Watch your thoughts, for they will become actions. Watch your actions, for they'll become . . . habits. Watch your habits, for they will forge your character. Watch your character, for it will make your destiny.

(Margaret Thatcher)

Moderation in temper is always a virtue, but moderation in principle is always a vice.

(Thomas Paine)

For more compelling Freedom quotations, see appendix 1f.

CHAPTER 2
EDUCATION

Communication is as old as humankind. One of the drivers of the development of language has been the passing on of encounters, thoughts, and opinions to better understand and improve one's own life experience.

Humans would not be what we are without those views and opinions shared around our proverbial campfires for thousands of years as we ponder these questions: *What was done correctly? What could have been done correctly? What should have been done differently?*

The aim is to learn. We cannot properly understand how to apply Critical Thinking to life's circumstances without first considering the foundation for human thought and advancement: Education.

Education is the beginning, the basis of human accountability and responsibility. One can presume Education in all its forms began at the earliest stages of human development. The family, the tribe, the hunt, the gathering of food, the development of community structures, all the way to modern pursuits in space, cyberspace, and artificial intelligence

(AI)—all embrace or evolve from the desire to seek to understand. That pursuit, at its root, is a thirst for Education and knowledge.

Education is the process of assisting the individual to acquire the tools necessary to understand, analyze, communicate, and ultimately to know. As such, the proper Education of our children is critical. They are the seed corn of humanity's future. Although we focus on the young, Education is an ongoing process that continues throughout one's life. We are continually learning, both passing on and being passed information.

A main goal of Education is the development of the individual's ability to think through issues and come to well-structured conclusions— the ability to Think Critically. A good Education is not indoctrination— which is mere rote memorization, regurgitation, and requires no actual application of the mind. As Albert Einstein put it, "Education is not the learning of facts, but the training of the mind to think." The purpose of Education is to give the individual useful tools so that options and alternatives can be considered for the most informed decision-making from the available information.

Education imparts knowledge and experience. This imparting process gives a society continuity, which implies succession and forward motion. You do not move forward if you continue to do what you have always done and think as you have always thought.

To understand Education, we must also understand what motivates and incentivizes individuals to learn. Education is the tool that provides the fuel to move forward. Such thought takes us from mere survival to self-actualization at the height of Maslow's hierarchy of needs.

1. Physiological

2. Safety

3. Belonging—social connection

4. Esteem

5. Self-actualization

Education and a common curriculum are the glue that binds us all together into families, communities, and societies, as they create the very fabric of society. Formal Education first appeared two thousand years before the birth of Christ. According to Robert Carneiro and Alexandra Draxler, society builds upon four common pillars of Education of learning to know, do, live together, and simply be. Over time it came to be believed that Education could be mass-produced to ensure certain goals, such as the following:

1. **Reading and Writing:** These were developed so that the legacy of experience could be permanently inscribed. The learning of the language in written, etched, or carved form ensured consistency in the passing of communication. The reading of the language was important because it allowed one to pass on and understand this information.

2. **Science and Mathematics:** This helped us multiply our time and resources to build the societies we see today. What once helped us improve our efficiency now helps us build skyscrapers and reach the moon and beyond. Science and Math have given us the tools for functioning, logical thinking, and development.

3. **History:** By recording our experiences and the losses and victories throughout the ages, we save ourselves centuries of time by simply remembering our mistakes. In doing so, we optimize our ability to grow without repeating our mistakes. Access to this information, for better or worse, mitigates errors and maximizes results. Besides the knowledge and understanding

of past mistakes, History also gives us examples of heroism, logic, wonderful discoveries, and great achievements. These become great inspirations for our personal and societal development.

4. **Religion and Faith:** By sharing the same understanding of the deep fundamental truths that tether together every aspect of our world, we have cohesion in our society. While indoctrination inevitably fails to ensure this cohesion, genuine Faith in something beyond our own lives helps keep us grounded in who is really in control in this world.

5. **The Arts:** Passing on our creativity and abilities to innovate and communicate in different ways not only gave us something to aspire to and hand down. It also resets expectations for what might come next. Each generation could then recreate on its own terms, building upon what had gone before, while working with and influencing other cultures as they influence us.

The purposes of Education are the following:

1. To develop the following abilities in people:

    a. Read

    b. Write

    c. Communicate

    d. Mathematically calculate

    e. Scientifically investigate

    f. Artistically express

2. To provide an explanation and tools for Critical Thinking.

3. To instill Religious Faith and Values that allow a society to remain grounded.

4. To teach History to give people an understanding of the past and present so that they can develop a consistent vision for the future while maintaining and improving the fabric of society and avoiding mistakes of the past.

5. To equip people with knowledge that allows them to compete effectively and globally.

6. To teach cultural literacy.

7. To train a work ethic of lifetime habits that cement a society.

8. To provide services only an educated population can provide (e.g., medical services, financial services, etc.).

9. To accomplish all this in order to prepare the next generation for leadership.

Education separates the privileged from the underprivileged. It has always been a tool employed by those in power to either narrow that gap or widen it, depending on their desires. It can be used to provide the continued support of cadres that kept the community, the Political System, the Economic System, and the religious system in place and to grow.

Education also helped sustain those in power through the selective application of its benefits. This was particularly true in the centuries before the printing press and the Gutenberg Bible. Before these innovations, whoever had their hands on a book or collection of books controlled access to information. Few could read, and there were significant restrictions for those who might have wanted to learn. Additionally, there was no mass printing back then.

Education supplies the basic building blocks for intellectual development, the foundation for all human advancements. The basic areas of Education listed below are important for a multitude of reasons and applications in everyday life—but very specifically for the sake of societal progress: specifically, the STEAM (Science, Technology, Engineering, Arts, and Math) pursuits that supply the necessary means for many technological advancements and thus for the progress of humanity.

The establishment of a quality Education should encourage all children to achieve their highest potential as individuals. It should promote them to serve as contributing citizens in a free society and successfully compete in a changing global marketplace.

Note well the word *compete*. Education is competitive when providers of Education have to try to outperform the existing standard and provide a better experience for students. Competitive educational systems provide continuously improving results. Conversely, when we eliminate competitive ideas and forums, we introduce the potential for governing structures to replace free inquiry with rote memorization—all to the detriment of society's advancement. We resign ourselves to the twin scourges of indoctrination and rote memorization. The first does not teach Critical Thinking, and the latter does not even promote learning. The goal of Education should be merit, achievement, and mastery of topics. Rote learning is detrimental to the advancement of humankind. We must Think Critically first before we can act rationally!

When allied with Critical Thinking, a true Education will trump indoctrination every time. Curiosity leads to creativity, which creates new solutions to problems—which, when allowed to be born, create competition in the marketplace of ideas. The fittest survive for the benefit of us all. Without competition, we produce bloated and complacent bureaucracies that resist change, we are stuck.

Critical Thinking, creativity, interpersonal skills, and a sense of social responsibility all influence success in life, work, and citizenship. (See also appendix 1e.) Understanding the History of humankind's development is also necessary to minimize the repetition of earlier mistakes. Throughout History, each period's educational system eventually failed. Regardless of the form of government, a functioning educational system naturally promotes the fundamental Freedom to Think, Question, and Speak. When we encourage these freedoms, we maximize our potential as a society and encourage our children to lead the way toward progress.

We do not know everything now, and we will not know everything in the future. Our only hope is to give our children the best understanding and framework possible so they can realize their full potential.

Our children *are* the future.

❋❋❋

Ray Dalio, founder of Bridgewater Strategies and a fifty-year student of geopolitics, draws a number of conclusions as to what enables a society to succeed or fail. He considers a number of conceiving factors that ensure a given society might succeed, and the very first is Education. The more educated a society is, the more likely it is to enjoy achievement, stability, economic development, and growth while acquiring wealth and power. Mr. Dalio includes innovation, technology, trade, competitiveness, economic output, and other areas as well, but he settles on Education as the foundational factor for success.

That is why educational policymakers should remember that curiosity, competition, and creativity are desirable in the schooling environment. The first thing Education should do is to inspire curiosity. Curiosity leads to creativity, which creates new solutions and reinforces the Critical Thinking process. The first question to ask then is how best to apply creativity to the schooling environment.

Unfortunately, bureaucracies often oppose doing things in new ways, which could put the system, of which they are part, at risk. But is Education for the students or for the administrators and their bureaucracy? All too often, the bureaucracy does what is best for itself instead of making improvements for the benefit of students. Fundamentally, more Critical Thinking is needed at all levels all the way up to the local school board level.

Second, a good educational system features competition. When there is competition, more than one system or apparatus exists. Therefore, different methods can be tried to develop a competitive advantage. Competition can be created within the bureaucracy or completely outside of it.

Let's consider those two alternatives. Competition within the educational bureaucracy does not currently exist. The Education industry in the United States is paralyzed by unions and groupthink. That paralysis destroys any meaningful competition that would push for educational enlightenment.

An example of this paralysis is the "No Child Left Behind" proposal under President George W. Bush. While focused on high-level testing and providing accountability for learning, the result further polarized the already-fractured Education industry. Teachers were and are not incentivized to be competitive. Advanced degrees and the number of teaching years of experience produce the matrix for salary compensation.

Teachers began to teach the test instead of imparting knowledge and Critical Thinking in an effort to help students identify and develop their God-given gifts.

Rote learning and memorization may, in fact, hurt the process of real Education. As nationally recognized Education expert Scott Looney discovered over time, "[T]he traditional assessment system—letter grades and Carnegie units [a time-based standard of student progress]—was getting in the way of giving kids feedback that applies to real-world, problem-solving, group-oriented work."

On the other hand, outside the bureaucracy, competition does exist among private Education choices. By allowing parents the freedom to choose their children's educational institutions and earmark money for their own children's institutions, healthy competition naturally arises among institutions. Each institution is then motivated to optimize its own Education format to be deemed the superior form of Education for parents. (See appendix 2a for more about introducing competition into our public school system.)

Any of the current Education models could be structured to employ creativity and competition, although some are more easily suited than others:

1. Public schools—available to all, publicly funded (see appendix 2a: Education—Internal Public School Competition Mechanics)

2. Charter schools—publicly funded with school vouchers, an independently run school of choice (parent-chosen)

3. Private schools—independently run, privately funded (primarily by parents of students)

4. Parochial schools—religiously affiliated private schools

5. Homeschools—privately run and cofunded by the student's family

Any successful educational model should prepare young people for life, work, and citizenship. It should help individuals to allegorically define the world around them so they can Think Critically about what is labeled *good*, *bad*, and *evil*. More importantly today than at any point in our History, it should help individuals prepare for rapid changes in vocations, stay current in technologies, and seize opportunities. Education profoundly shapes mankind's future. We can choose to infuse it with dynamic qualities, or we can plod along, hoping against hope that using the same process repeatedly will lead to different and improved results.

Unfortunately, certain theories being pushed today emphasize reducing requirements for students. This is not a prescription for better results. The blame for the recent decline in the quality of Education lies squarely at the feet of those who support lowering the bar. This process cheapens the efforts and causes inferior results that put any society at risk in its ability to compete internationally.

While we want to make great Education available to all, if we lower the standard to make our results equal, we will only lose our exceptional students and fail to compete on the world's stage. Some individuals are motivated to achieve superior results. Others have no interest in a high level of achievement and merely coast. Our goal should be to allow each student to reach their full potential, not reduce the results so that every student is equal but mediocre. A curious and competitive educational system will naturally develop an equality of opportunity.

Finally, we hold the keys to the kingdom within Education. Our evaluation of teachers and administrative leaders in Education has used faulty criteria with little consideration for leadership skills. We seem to select individuals who have shown the greatest intellectual talent. However, a poor leader with great intellectual talent can be a disaster in a leadership position. We, therefore, believe that testing for natural leadership attributes should be a fundamental criterion for selection by institutions, universities, corporations, divisions, and teams in selecting individuals. Those testing with the highest natural attributes hold the key to our society's ongoing success. And this all flows from an excellent educational environment.

In the words of former Berkshire Hathaway Vice Chairman Charlie Munger, "I prefer inequality to poverty."

Education is *not* indoctrination. It is society's preparation of its children for their future responsibilities. Competition in Education creates creative, critical thinkers—what society needs. Critical Thinking must be the ultimate goal of any Education system: to create an environment that optimizes equal opportunity for all students instead of mandating equal results.

> *Education is not the learning of facts,*
> *but the training of the mind to think.*
>
> (ALBERT EINSTEIN)

> *The mediocre teacher tells. The good*
> *teacher explains. The superior teacher*
> *demonstrates. The great teacher inspires.*
>
> (WILLIAM ARTHUR WARD)

CHAPTER 3
RELIGION, FAITH, AND VALUES

We all have spiritual needs. These needs develop into Values that are reflected in our lives. An unfortunate consequence is that our discussions on Values are often hotly contested depending on our religious worldview.

Religion, belief in deities, or the development of Faith structures has been a fixture of humanity for millenia. It initially served as a means of rationalizing forces beyond human explanation, things that had the power to do the unexpected and seemingly unexplainable. Often, these beings were tied to issues like storms, fertility, death, and war. (Notable examples include Baal, Ra, Zeus, Hades, Mars, Apollo, Thor, Oden, and more.) Interestingly, these are some of the issues we still wrestle with as a society today.

Many Religions were polytheistic and political. Nations were essentially closed societies in which civil and religious obedience were identical. All law was divine law and was imposed upon defeated enemies. Political authority came directly from the deity or deities worshipped by the various societies and civilizations.

The deities required the obeisance of man. With proper behavior, it was assumed, the god(s) would look favorably on humankind and withhold wrath. However, worship and belief evolved over time. With each new society came the rise of a new Religion with new religious texts revered as the truth. Some global Religions promote the need to love and respect other followers of their Faith, regardless of cultural differences. As this happened, they grew into the Religions we see today.

Most Religions also assume they are exclusively correct. Their understanding and teaching of what they believe is fundamentally important to them because that belief underpins their whole worldview. Like water to a fish, we often fail to understand how our deeply held beliefs touch every aspect of our lives.

Ideally, we presently recognize Religion as a value system expressing the wishes of the divine. A consequence of this is the need to see one's own worldview triumph. All religious institutions, even including some Christian institutions, have forced their belief structure upon other civilizations at times, often with disastrous results. Other times we have seen religious symbolism or teaching taken out of context and perverted to support evil institutions. However idealistic we may be, we must acknowledge the friction and seek to avoid the missteps of our collective past.

Let us keep in mind that before and after the birth of Christ, many parts of the world worshipped pagan entities, spirits, and even nature. Even Moses, after coming face-to-face with God himself, was confronted with the Israelites worshipping a golden idol when he returned down from Mount Sinai. Nevertheless, the lesson of the story is clear: The temptation and the basic urge or need to worship something more powerful than us is universal. Humans yearn for the presence of support, comfort, security, and guidance in an uncomfortable existence and an unpredictable world—a way to rationalize the inexplicably good and the inexplicably bad.

As stated earlier, some religious factions desire to pose their Religion as the superior one or as the only one that matters. By this, we mean, the only one through which one can ascend into Paradise after death. For centuries, people born into these Religions followed blindly because it was all they knew. They never had the opportunity to exercise Critical Thinking because they were told it was the only option. Why question it? In many societies, asking questions became an easy way to find yourself in a colosseum, on an altar, or put to death. Critical Thinking was silenced so the Religion could endure.

Every person realizes there are things we do not understand. In Plato's "Allegory of the Cave," he described men who had always lived in a cave and watched shadow puppets on the wall. It was all they knew. They had no concept of questioning what they were seeing. But even so, they still knew there was something more beyond what they were physically seeing.

The human focus on Religion is interesting. Two central aspects stand out: First, seeking a Religion to adhere to on earth is part of our earthly experience. We try to understand our Religion and live according to its teachings. Often, this leads to separate groups coming into conflict with one another. Some have tried to bridge this divide. Some realize that while we live on earth, we attempt to live under a value system we individually accept in applying our freedom of Religion. This group realizes that they can never speak for God because they don't possess absolute knowledge of his will. So we attempt to live godly lives such that our God may accept us into heaven by applying his will.

It should seem obvious, therefore, that the great mistake of those seeking to *force* others to join their Religion is that salvation is not up to us because the decision is God's and God's alone. No Religion should expressly advocate the need to be approved by man.

There is no checklist for action determined by humans on earth to achieve a passing grade to earn acceptance by that heavenly power. Earning one's way into what we call heaven is not feasible because, at the end of the day, it attempts to put the human in charge of the checklist. Anyone believing they have the right to pass such judgment on earth is naive. We will never know just how God determines the human soul's access to heaven without hearing from him directly. Since the beginning, hundreds of Religions have sprung up to answer this universal, commonsense question. It is only the eyes of God that matter when our eternal existence comes to an end. Why humans worry about supplying answers to this important but unknowable question amazes us. Since we can't know the answer by definition, it would seem that our only choice is to live a consistent life, being thoughtful of the rest of humankind.

It is nonsensical to think that a human can determine another person's salvation. Cicero once noted how, by using mere Common Sense, all people know that they fell from God's good graces. He also noted that since then, even the best of us are unable to return to that level of bliss without divine intervention. However, in 44 BC, Cicero stopped just shy of reasoning that God would come down to us to save us. He did not think that the only way we could be reconciled with God was for him to act first. No single human could let you in or keep you out if God wanted you. A lifetime later, Christ was born with a similar message.

Let us remember that the Pilgrims' main goal of their 1620 voyage was religious freedom, which we continue to share to this day. During the American Great Awakenings, a revolutionary concept emerged that God wants individuals to act *voluntarily* and in a holy fashion due to their love for him. Taking the ideals of the Protestant Reformation, the Awakenings emphasized how free choice was essential to creating willing disciples. This ideal eventually factored into the American Revolution and the emphasis on freedom of Religion.

Most Religions have value systems. The Golden Rule and the ethics of reciprocity, or something like it, are recurring themes. Do unto others as you would have them do unto you. These Values seem like Common Sense. Yet our natural default is to be more self-centered. Religion helps bridge the gap between these isolated individuals and converge their goals towards one end—*community*.

Without the Value Systems that have emanated from the different Religions, would humankind have made the advances we have today? Would Asia, the Middle East, Europe, or North America be what it is today without those Values and beliefs? Is it not beneficial to utilize the major religious teachings to determine a path of harmonious coexistence?

Religion and foundational morals are fundamental to the development of humankind. This progress could not have occurred at the rate it did without thought, a questioning mind, and freedom of speech. Religion gives clarity of purpose. We certainly would not have the remarkable Declaration of Independence (1776), the Articles of Confederation (1781), the United States Constitution (1787), and the subsequent Bill of Rights (1791) without Religion. After all, what would they protect if they had not enshrined the freedom of Religion?

Man has developed over millennia. That being said, the development occurred much more rapidly after the invention of the printing press and the governmental focus on the individual's freedoms that came through the development of the Western man. We ascribe the increasing pace of development to the freedoms ensured in constitutional structures in Western Europe and the United States, along with their Judeo-Christian Values as the forces of influence enhancing that rate of development in Western civilization.

That raises the question of what Judeo-Christian Values are. Dennis Prager of Prager University states there are ten in his video "What Are Judeo-Christian Values (which are the moral foundation of Western civilization)?"

1. There is one God, which was introduced by the Hebrew Bible.

2. There are objective moral truths. Without God, there are no moral truths, only moral opinions.

3. Good and evil are the same for all people.

4. God is the source of our rights.

5. The human being is made in the image of God; therefore, every human life is precious, and race is of no significance because God has no race.

6. The world is based on a divine order that is based on distinctions:

    a. God and man

    b. God and nature

    c. Man and woman

    d. Human and animal

    e.   Good and evil

7. Man is not basically good. We need God-based rules to keep us from our natural inclinations.

8. Natural inclinations are a poor moral guide.

9. Human beings have free will and are, therefore, responsible for how they behave.

10. The Ten Commandments are the core of Judeo-Christian Values.

The ultimate embodiment of those Values is in the United States, as displayed in a seal for the United States designed by Thomas Jefferson and Benjamin Franklin. It depicts Israel being led out of Egypt, just as they believed that God led America out of Europe.

To reinforce those concepts, this quote from Margaret Thatcher is useful: "The truths of Judeo-Christian tradition are infinitely precious, not only . . . because they are true, but also because they provide the moral impulse which alone can lead to that peace . . . for which we all long."

In addition, in an article by Mikayla Hendrick, Jordan Peterson once said, "We've come to a time when we have to understand what the stories our culture is predicated on actually mean." Peterson's point was that we have, "arguably the greatest culture on earth . . . If you want to keep the culture, keep the story. If you want to keep the story, you have to keep God."

And while Religion can provide excellent rules for humankind to live by, it has also been the excuse for chaotic and grotesque atrocities. Even though we believe Religion or spirituality has been a net positive for humankind's development, we would be remiss not to point out the damage that the improper application of Religion has done: human sacrifice, violent impositions of specific Religions upon entire societies, and individuals believing that they have the cultural authority to decide whether another lives or dies without due process. These historical examples of villainy demonstrate the potential evil that wrongly applied Religion can do within societies.

Despite the evil implementation of religious and totalitarian structures and activities, it seems most humans are drawn to Religion and Values. Why is that? The answer is surprisingly simple. In the end, we are all driven to Faith for the purpose of guiding us through life.

Human beings are relational, emotional, and spiritual creatures. We can also be logical. That said, we often struggle to bridge this gap between the left brain and the right brain. Our Values and religious views help us do that. We seek a construct to explain the logic and illogic of actions and to provide comfort in death and continuity after death. Throughout History, traditional or long-serving Values have played a pivotal role in providing a stable and moral foundation for societal development, acknowledging the importance of cultural continuity and consistency in cultural behavior. Despite the hijackings of the past, we all recognize the potential for Religion to promote peace.

There is something inescapable about Religion. It has existed since the dawn of humankind. Regardless of whether people liked the concept of Religion, every society has needed to worship something. Even Communism, as Marx explained, was predicated on worshipping the state in the absence of a god, essentially state-inspired self-worship.

What compelled all societies over time to create a form of Faith, a thing(s) or spirit(s) to be worshipped? The need for this structure of Religion and ultimate devotion is intrinsic to the human condition and, consequently, inherent to societies' Value Systems.

But we must be careful. Absolute Faith without compassion, without governance, without filters, without a logical foundation will never outrun the drive for power and evil. The ends of one's Faith will always be determined by the foundation.

Without Religion, humanity would never have achieved anything short of nihilism. Nihilism is the theory of life where a person rejects basic concepts of morality, knowledge, and meaning. Essentially, it operates in the assumption of a vacuum, where there are no objective truths. The relative nature of nihilism often leads people to grapple with a deep feeling of meaninglessness, hopelessness, and ultimately, worthlessness.

Thankfully, most people believe there is a story or purpose to this world. We surely would not have achieved any of humankind's many victories without Faith in something. But humanity's basest desires and drives, self-serving actions, and desire for omnipotence and control often overpower the holistic good that Religion might otherwise offer the world.

Religion promotes our desire to belong, to be part of a group, to be part of something with shared beliefs. Individuals' desire to organize, balance, and accommodate is important to ensure that belonging does not turn into or mean exclusion, domination, or worse. Governments often tie themselves to religious Values in an effort to tap into this feeling of belonging. People who feel like they belong through a Value System are less inclined to hurt their neighbors. They become team players instead of a party of one against the world.

This general tenet is accounted for in Rousseau's idea of a social contract. The government attains its right to exist and to govern by "the consent of the governed." Specifically, Rousseau identified three stages of humanity's organizational development:

1. The state of nature where man is free and independent;

2. Society, in which man is oppressed and dependent on others; and

3. The state under the social contract in which man becomes free through obligation.

Freedom and equality flow from these propositions and a religious Value System. Our Founding Fathers, as expressed in our founding documents, understood that man's right to both freedom and equality was only possible while living under the just rule of law. For example, the Declaration of Independence states: " . . . all men are created equal, that they are endowed by their Creator with certain unalienable Rights . . ."

Further, any lack of transparency and consistency undermines the value systems passed down through time through religious and spiritual beliefs and ideologies. Because of this, faithful interpretation and execution of the laws is a necessity. When our institutions don't carry out the letter of the law or honor their responsibilities effectively, transparently, and consistently, our social contract begins to weaken.

Where there is a question of the faithfulness of our institutions carrying out their responsibilities, one of the most important things we can do is to modify our mechanisms so that our ability to clearly see failure, stagnation, and corruption is uninhibited. Such is central to creating the desired effect of ever strengthening the fabric of society, which is by itself a huge societal goal enhanced and strengthened by its moral fiber from religious Values. Further streamlining and simplifying societal Values and laws make it easier for any society to grasp its responsibilities.

One way of interpreting Rousseau's social contract is that the individual, in agreeing to be protected by the society they are a part of, gives up violence to realize the more democratized structural benefits of an organized society.

By doing so, the individual enters a social contract where they agree to accept the current mechanisms, rules, laws, and regulations they will live under while being able to use the available stated and accepted channels for altering those same mechanisms, rules, laws, and regulations for society's further improvement. Optimally, the individual possesses the freedom of thought and of speech whereby, in a peaceful fashion, they may express their thoughts, questions, and ideas.

Another way of describing the concept is as a determination to preserve human freedoms in a world where people are increasingly interdependent upon one another. They must use their Critical Thinking skills to improve their articles of mutual governance for a more sovereign and successful nation.

Our innate desire to be wanted, to belong, to fit in comes from our spiritual desire for relationships. All lasting Religions depend on a tradition of relationships.

For the Norwegians, Egyptians, Greeks, Carthaginians, and Romans, their gods were people constantly at odds with one another. They would kill, bargain, and even pillage and rape as they wanted. This was not conducive to a relational society. The Romans adopted the system from the East of worshipping their leader after a while, and society would change based on the leader.

Then Christianity came and introduced millions to the concept of a single God who was, in and of himself, relational. A triune God who is always Father, Son, and Holy Spirit (a friend closer than a brother) and yet is still one single essence. This radically changed how people saw each other. Slaves and masters were reconciled. Racial minorities and majorities began to erase histories of prejudice. Eventually, even Roman emperors conceded to this change in the course of History.

Fast-forward almost two thousand years, and we can see this change of course in the human story still running its course. Rousseau, Locke, and the Founding Fathers took this concept of relationship and created a new philosophy. The social contract is a relationship. That relationship spawned our Values as a society.

The understanding of human law is enhanced as a function of Rousseau's social contract. The connection and tension between the individual and Society mandate the incorporation of laws that are consistent and based on eternal truths. Short-term, variable, changeable postulates that fit today, but lack integrity and gravitas, are not sustaining or advancing. Laws are the civil and criminal responses to the need for society and the individual to live in harmony. When the individual or society acts without accountability or responsibility, laws serve to rebalance the equation between the individual and society.

Accountability and responsibility are bylaws of this construct; without them, the individual and society can run wild to the detriment of those living within society and also to the detriment of the legitimacy of the society itself. There are limits. Court decisions do not pass spiritual judgment. Courts attempt to protect society from various forms of wrongdoing while also remaining cognizant of the individual's personal freedoms and their personal pursuit of happiness. If one does not agree with a law or laws as they exist, then they must follow the mechanisms provided to a society in their constitution to have those changes accepted and incorporated.

For society to function, one must acknowledge that most members of this or any society voluntarily make contributions of their labor, intellect, or capital voluntarily to allow society to function as it is intended.

We learn as we earn, which allows us to reinforce our self-identity and self-worth. The individual's earned and independent journey, rife with achievement and experience, benefits society and our governing structures, even as the rights of the individual provide the rationale for governance and shape the design and control over that very government in the first place.

For those who do not necessarily believe in organized Religion, per se, is it not worthwhile to have some long-lived thesis that bestows humanity's lessons (e.g., the Golden Rule, the Ten Commandments, etc.) on how to live and coexist? Society needs a Value System with which to ground itself.

Value Systems are the glue that binds individuals into a cohesive set of common beliefs. And here we see the Value of Education that provides the tools for the individual to be adequately prepared or educated to comprehend the complexity of how a society can and should function, even as the individual, by definition, properly focuses on the pursuit of self-interest, competitive pursuits, and governance oversight.

Trouble develops when Religion merges with the government structures to undermine the social contract for their own purposes. Examples are replete in History to include theocracies, communism, fascism, socialism, and monarchies that relied upon the churches to suppress opinion and maintain dominance.

A classic historical example of this government overreach was Hitler's use of the term "the big lie": "People can be induced to believe a colossal lie because they would not believe that someone could have the impudence to distort the truths so infamously."

In talking about Religion, we are talking about the basic human drive to understand what is beyond ourselves and our existence. There are shared underlying foundational articles and messages of Faith that unite many of the world's Religions. There are common beliefs in those matters, actions, and thoughts that serve more to bind us together than to differentiate and drive us apart.

Do we not see then a way to incorporate in our daily lives the spiritual teachings of centuries and millennia that can clarify action? We need the understanding of what separates church and state over time and what guarantees the sanctity of the individual in the face of a state that can demand obeisance and deprive the individual of all the rights of self-governance.

All conversations become direct and, indeed, simple if this purpose is kept in mind. In the focus of giving, we believe we find the greatest receipt of all—happiness in finding a value system that allows us to live harmoniously with our fellow humans while we pursue our careers and love for our families. Religion, Faith, and the attendant Values can assist every society in reaching its full potential. Religion teaches that there is much more that binds us together than separates us.

There is something inexorable about Religion. It has existed since the dawn of humankind. We are at a loss in all of life without a coherent religious foundation. Period.

Furthermore, without Faith and Values, we cannot have a lasting and persistent need to Think Critically. What compelled all societies over time to create a form of Faith, a thing (or things) to be worshipped? The need for this structure of Religion and ultimate devotion is intrinsic to the human condition and, consequently, inherent to a society's Value System.

But we must be careful. Absolute Faith without compassion, without governance, without filters, without a logical foundation will never outrun the drive for power and evil. Nevertheless, it is not for us to tell others how to apply their spiritual focus. Whether their focus has been well applied can only be determined by God. Thus, freedom of Religion should be an inalienable right for all human beings informed by their personal Value System and their personal spiritual beacon.

The focus of Faiths and Religions worldwide should be to encourage a shared, harmonious, and thoughtful life with all humans, regardless of alternative beliefs or claims. The individual is free to be godless, but they are not free to force their godlessness on others. Meanwhile, the respect and love for others that Religion engenders is a key principle for progress. Religion develops Faith, and from those two flows a Value System. Humankind in true self-governance requires the grounding found in a well-developed Value System, which is necessary to successfully apply the governance activities across all of society.

CHAPTER 4
HISTORY

History should be the factual study of the past. Unfortunately, this may not always be the case. An accurate description of what factually occurred is all that is needed for a proper telling of History. But humans naturally seek to communicate and help explain *how* and *why* things occur.

Information can be used, interpreted, and presented as factual even when it has been altered. The person telling the story often applies his or her perspective to the narrative, which risks misleading and even deceiving the reader. However, a properly trained student has all the tools he or she needs to spot these biases.

To understand History, people must be literate and embrace Critical Thinking. By properly applying one's Education and religious imperatives, people can correct perspectives on past events and live life according to their most deeply held beliefs. But Critical Thinking must always be part of the study.

The study of History gives humankind the ability to avoid repeating mistakes. If we find that an approach has been tried and doesn't work, then we can try alternative solutions with greater understanding and knowledge. Every period of time or epoch in History represents human experimentation with Religion, Faith, and Values; Political Systems; and Economic Systems as developed up to that time in various locations around the world. These "experiments" themselves are History, and History helps guide humankind forward, if we will take those lessons to heart. Critical Thinking and analysis of those historical events help us learn from those "experiments."

In some cases, where the current conditions do not perfectly match historical conditions, we must make an inference. It is in attempting to find the best answers, rather than being driven off the correct path toward a specifically desired outcome, that Critical Thinking becomes truly "critical."

When people attempt to erase the past or contort our understanding of what occurred, they do a disservice to us all. The removal of statues, the renaming of military bases, and the name-changing of sports teams are all efforts of distortion and canceling the past. They blind us to the pitfalls of generations past. And why? Because they want to present a different face of reality. What they forget is that reality hits hardest when we don't see it coming. So accuracy and historical truth are important for optimal preparation to minimize surprise and even shock in the future.

Critical Thinking and integrity of thought are the foundation of being true to oneself and society. Without the ability to Think Critically about the lessons of History, individuals become mere sheep following shepherds with their own agendas. Historical literacy and the study of History are crucial components of knowing what came before, understanding its applicability to what and where we are now, and moving toward where we want to go.

History is the study of human responsibility, accountability, community, family, and societal norms—in essence, the very fabric of society. It allows us to better understand the intersectionality of global societies, the migrations, trade, and thoughts of people around the world. Furthermore, it helps us understand our own Faith and beliefs by applying our worldview to events spanning millions or billions of lives and a world full of scenarios.

History bestows perspective on the present, helping us to understand our own times and ideas. Without that perspective, we as a society are limited to being judged only in the context of present ideologies and political aims and interests.

History bent to some other aim becomes propaganda. Propaganda's willful distortion of History in service of an ideological cause can confront humanity at any time. Recall George Orwell's *1984* and his description of what happens when societies abandon belief in objective historical truth:

> The Party could thrust its hand into the past and say of this or that event, "it never happened," that surely was more terrifying than mere torture and death. And if all others accepted the lie in the Party (all records told the same tale), then the lie passed into history and became the truth. "Who Controls The Past," ran the party slogan, "Controls The Future: Who Controls The Present Controls The Past."

A lack of Critical Thinking prevents people from learning from History. When we actually engage with History, we must evaluate our belief structure to see if it is misleading us. If we are guided by our beliefs, then we cannot simply be content to observe History happening in front of us and expect true progress to occur. We must look to perspectives beyond our own time to discover timeless truths.

This is the gift of History. We can observe it as it moves forward. We may determine what it means to our times, or to the future, and whether it reflects historical truth. But have we analyzed that History deeply enough to truly comprehend it?

You can observe an atomic bomb and know that it exploded. You can observe its strength, its destructive power, and its operation. But have you understood why the bomb went off? What actually happened internally, second by second? Who set it off, and for what purposes?

When we apply Critical Thinking to History, we do not stop at the pamphlet level of History. We must delve deep into the thoughts, experiences, and beliefs that propelled History forward. With deep reflection, we realize the reality of historical events and mine the historical truths.

Did Winston Churchill's belief in the supremacy of the British Empire, as well as his desire to force Turkey out of World War I, result in the disaster at Gallipoli? Was there a backup plan if the battleships could not navigate the Dardanelles? Did their captains alter the battle plans? Why was the operation not aborted?

By searching out the errors leading up to a tragedy, we seek to avoid such failures moving forward. Churchill understood this in the 1940s as he used the lessons learned from that event in his past to alter how he defended against a world war. But we cannot all expect to have the costly lesson Churchill had at Gallipoli. Instead, we should seek to learn from the same experience he had to avoid such a high toll in the future.

Likewise, the bombing of Pearl Harbor was a decisive moment leading to America's entry into World War II. But was the tragedy of that day necessary? Were there not enough indications of impending

Japanese action after America embargoed Japan's oil eighteen months earlier? Where was the effective decision-making during those eighteen months? It was a singular commitment to stay out of the war without critical analysis and thought of all alternatives and the consequences of the potential choice of each alternative. Political bias overwhelmed those potential consequences of alternative choice.

Once we grow our ability to Think Critically, there is no end to the questions we can seek to comprehend. But when we fail to reflect on History, we fail to realize that certain endeavors have been tried before—and failed.

For example, what are the economic determinants that drive an individual or group toward the pursuit of absolute power? Do they believe they can control their economy? Surely, the marketplace is too complex to be centrally planned. Individuals make their own consumption and purchasing decisions where mass valuation meets price point discovery in the competitive marketplace. A market of millions and billions of microdecisions does not allow for a command economy. History has proven this. And yet for hundreds of years, the world over, those in power attempted to control these very instruments of economic and political authority.

Where is the Critical Thinking? What are we doing to combat and defeat these destructive but ultimately fruitless efforts? As we approach the end of the first century of applied nuclear power, do we have the luxury of wishful thinking?

Another fine example is the question of international conflicts. Historically speaking, what is the purpose of international conflict and war? What is the purpose of conquering and dominating others? How do we reconcile hegemony with the geographic and demographic rights of countries to exist without domination or submission?

A modern spin on this classic question could be these questions: What specifically is China's goal in its push for world domination? What does China hope to achieve, and has China thought through what would be required to be successful in such a mission? Can it be accomplished? Does not communistic thought impact discussion, comment, and the use of Critical Thinking freely? What is the compelling imperative here? How can the study of Critical Thinking, Education, Religion, History, Politics, and Economics help the world reconcile itself with these conflicting thoughts that the efforts of communist China pose?

The History of humankind is full of stories of imperfection. We often learn more from what we did wrong than what we did right. When we eliminate historical acknowledgments of the past as presented in statues, buildings, and plaques, we ultimately only harm our own collective memory. Though the individuals referred to or depicted may have had major personal faults or even represent an evil period or age, we know that at some point in time, they played a formative role for better or worse.

In some cases, those depicted have been heroic personalities; in other cases, they have been incomprehensibly criminal thugs. That said, society yearns for History, for remembrance—we yearn to know. In keeping with the lessons of Orwell's *1984*, it is how we frame the events of that past that is important.

There have been many interesting personalities throughout History. Some are true giants. While we must recognize the historical truth of historical figures and events, we should also take intentional note of how these people and moments have brought us to and shaped our reality. It does no good to simply theorize about what needs to happen in the future. To benchmark our progress and to have a positive impact on humankind's development, we must recognize the errors and evils of the past

From the Greek city-states to the Roman Empire, from the feudal monarchies of Europe to the industrial and technological advancements of the nineteenth and twentieth centuries, we have myriads of lessons to learn. We see humankind's questioning of institutions, the rise of broad societal Education, the creative mass production of products and services, and the allocation of individual resources of time and money reflecting their own preferences and optimizations.

We see that it is the Education of the masses that has freed creativity and allowed development at an ever-increasing pace. That, in itself, is a large lesson to be recognized. In earlier epochs, Education had been limited to the privileged. One of the purposes of limiting Education was to maintain the very concept of privilege for the elite.

Educational, religious, and political structures in earlier centuries were contrived and concurrently employed for the maintenance of this privilege. With Education becoming a universal right in most societies today, the battle for privilege was democratized by the overlapping spheres of competitive opportunities. It is this right to Education that empowers such a large portion of humanity to develop their potential more fully in the marketplace of decisions. Favorable evolution occurs through competition. It is within this competitive environment that societies at large determine what are the best Values.

There remain many examples of bad human behavior that continue today. But by understanding what is working and what has worked throughout History, humankind can evolve structures, laws, and regulations to protect the vast population. Then and only then can we properly amend the social contracts of our societies as Rousseau so well described in *The Social Contract* (1762).

For example, we are personally from America. Our societal fabric was woven together through the Protestant Reformation, the Great Awakenings, the American Revolution, and the continued march toward a better tomorrow. But our experience as a country truly began when we adopted the Declaration of Independence.

In a defiant moment, we as a people looked at the period of abuses we had experienced and applied the patterns of History to our circumstances. The clear result was that we were on the path to further despotism. First, we spoke with our voices. Then, we spoke with our actions.

The Declaration of Independence contains one of the best summations of the principles that laid the foundation for our social contract:

> When in the Course of human Events, it becomes necessary for one People to dissolve the Political Bands that have connected them with another, and to assume among the Powers of the Earth, the separate and equal Station to which the Laws of Nature and of Nature's God entitle them, a decent Respect to the Opinions of Mankind requires that they should declare the causes which impel them to the Separation.
>
> We hold these truths to be self-evident, that all men are created equal, they are endowed by their Creator with certain unalienable Rights, that among these are Life, Liberty, and the Pursuit of Happiness. That to secure these Rights, Governments are instituted among Men, deriving their just powers from the consent of the Governed, that whenever any Form of Government becomes destructive of those Ends, it is the Right of the People to alter or to abolish it, and to institute

new Government, laying its Foundation on such Principles, and organizing its Powers in such Form, as to them shall seem most likely to affect their Safety and Happiness. Prudence, indeed, will dictate that Governments long established should not be changed for light and transient Causes; and accordingly, all Experience hath shown, that Humankind is more disposed to suffer, while Evils are sufferable, than to right themselves by abolishing the Forms to which they are accustomed. But when a long Train of Abuses and Usurpations, pursuing invariably the same Object, evinces a Design to reduce them under absolute Despotism, it is their right, it is their duty, to throw off such Government, and to provide new Guards for their future security

This profound passage recognizes that it is necessary to clearly state the underlying reasoning for such a serious undertaking. Furthermore, it was only through a deep understanding of History that the founders ultimately decided to act. In doing so, they brilliantly created our country.

Most modern societies have an origin story. But many have begun to question whether they approve of or want to remember their origins. The mistake many make is to attempt to erase what has been done. This is impossible. The History remains; only your perspective changes. We can either learn from the past or ignore it at the peril of repeating it.

In America, the other core document of our social contract is the Constitution itself. The purpose of the United States Constitution was to create a governing document that freed the citizens of the country to pursue their own individual dreams for the betterment of their society while not disenfranchising or infringing upon the lives of their fellow citizens. If a noncitizen arrives in another country, they are subject to the laws and regulations of that country, but without a voice. Individuals have a voice in the countries they are citizens of, but their voices are of little concern to countries they freely visit. It is not the right of noncitizens to tell citizens what they must do to facilitate their concerns and desires.

Our Founding Fathers laid the groundwork for the nation's citizens to realize the importance of their freedoms, especially to think, question, and speak, in constructing their future. And with their constitutional freedoms came the burden to protect them, to be ever vigilant in the creation and application of laws and regulations.

CHAPTER 5
POLITICAL SYSTEMS

P olitical Systems are measured by their ability to meet the demands placed upon them. They reflect the spectrum of basic modes of self-governance and monarchy to the complex democratic and totalitarian systems of today. Political Systems also provide the delineation of boundaries that help define countries, states, and regions.

No matter what civilization or society is mentioned and discussed, all must meet the needs of their people, or they will wither and die over time.

Every successful Political System balances between societal benefits and communal self-preservation on the one hand and the focus on the individual's rights to create an optimal environment for the pursuit of self-interest on the other. Political Systems based upon power and fear are short-lived, giving way to yet another power that takes over. This is observable as a conflicted nature and studied by biologist E. O. Wilson. The competing pulls of selfishness and altruism (sin and virtue) are essential elements of the human condition. Balancing these impulses makes a political structure stable, while an imbalance over time destabilizes it. There is almost always a stubborn tendency to favor one's own group over others, a tendency that needs to be overcome.

Anarchy and chaos can occur when Political Systems fail. When institutional structures and processes fail to resolve conflicts of various demands among its citizens, and when they are viewed as unresponsive to those very members of society, the institutional structure is often unable to maintain itself.

As Canadian-American political theorist David Easton has said, "A political system can be designated as the interactions through which values are authoritatively allocated for a society." Here we see the influence of the culture of a society and its belief structure. One cannot escape the integration of politics as structure and system with the needs of the individual.

All civilizations and societies, however ancient or old or new, require structure to attend to the needs of the members of that civilization or society. This empirical fact leads one to observe that throughout the History of humankind, consistent tension has existed between stable and unstable Political Systems and structures. A stable Political System is one that survives through crisis without internal warfare.

Hundreds of years before Christ, Aristotle indicated that "when there is no middle class, and the poor greatly exceed in number, troubles arise, and the state soon comes to an end." A stable Political System is one in which the middle class is in control and outnumbers both of the other classes.

Systems that are governed by ruling elites have historically worked (for a period of time) until the composition of the elite class leads to alienation of the masses and political change (usually violent). An example of this could be when most of society becomes separated or estranged from the elite and feels little, if any, connection to the decision-making process.

At the dawn of civilization, we had to survive as hunters and gatherers in small family groups connected to tribal structures made up of multiple families. We hunted for food wherever it was found and survived and thrived based on the learned skills. These skills included primitive toolmaking, communal activities that supported the structure of daily life, and divided labor to effectively utilize the skill sets of different individuals. Our primate ancestors already evidenced social and political skills as they lived as families within a band of society.

These systems helped us endure those early brutal centuries. Over the course of time, the human race found itself scattered across six continents, with thousands of dialects and a multitude of cultures. Such global human journeys were not aimless but driven by the need for food and receptive soil for agriculture. They discovered better or different climates depending on their purpose. The further they explored, the less competition they incurred from other tribal groups. Surviving the journeys required some form of organization and political structure.

Civilizations did eventually stop their migration, and the development of civilization ensued. Rules for social intercourse were adopted, and the mechanics of activity for economic exchange within a political structure were devised.

All civilizations share certain characteristics:

1. Development of urban settlements

2. Cultivation of land

3. Trade between farmers, fishers, and traders

4. Shared communication strategies

5. Administration and division of people into social and economic classes

Most societies go a step further and institute infrastructure and cultural exchange; encounter intercourse with other civilizations through trade, conflict, and exploration; and establish government structures intended to manage and maintain continuity. (See also appendix 5b.)

Critical Thought (including trial and error) drove the development of systems adopted by the civilization, making these choices. People modified and adjusted structures over time as life evolved day to day. Over the generations, modified Political Systems appeared in response to the needs of individuals and groups. But Political Systems can be both stable and unstable. Thus, Critical Thinking is vital as a defense against societal chaos and anarchy.

Typically, there are five primary types of Political Systems:

1. Democratic

2. Authoritarian

3. Totalitarian

4. Hybrids

5. Anarchic regimes

Democracies can be a pure democracy with the simple rule of the majority. Or they may be further refined to a constitutional republic to avoid the tyranny of the majority: a republic, per se, with elected representatives and a president.

Authoritarian regimes reject democracy and political plurality and use strong central power to preserve the status quo. The state structure can be autocratic or oligarchic, but the rule of force is a major component.

Totalitarian regimes are a form of government that prohibits opposition and outlaws the political claims of individuals and any group opposition to the state. The public and private spheres of society are all subject to total control by the state. Such systems become dictatorships, which invariably include control of all media.

Monarchies are built around the rule of a monarch (and often their extended family) as the head of state for life or until abdication. Typically, they are generational affairs, with children (typically firstborn sons) inheriting political authority after the death of the parent. The definition of *hybrid* can apply to states in an incomplete transition from authoritarian to democratic rule. These often cross over definitional boundaries and occur often in developing countries.

Democracies represent state power vested in the citizenry or general population of the state, respecting the rights of freedom of thought. They attempt to guarantee civil liberties, human rights, and competitive elections to provide continuity for governance.

In 1787, Alexander Fraser Tytler, Lord Woodhouselee, a Scotsman, commented on the new US experiment as a democracy. He said these powerful words:

> A democracy cannot exist as a permanent form of government. It can only exist until the voters discover that they can vote themselves largesse from the public treasury. From that moment on, the majority always votes for the candidates promising the most benefits from the public treasury, with the result that a democracy always collapses over loose fiscal policy, always followed by a dictatorship. The average age of the world's greatest civilizations has been about 200 years. Those

nations have progressed through this sequence: From bondage to spiritual faith; From spiritual faith to great courage; From great courage to liberty; From liberty to abundance; From abundance to selfishness; From selfishness to apathy; From apathy to dependence; From dependence back into bondage. (Cycle of Democracy, 1770)

His prediction has proven astonishingly accurate, with the last step yet to be played out in the United States. It may already be too late.

What then are the signs of system change and transition to political collapse? Is the regression from just and desired governance to corrupt domination inevitable? In the words of Lord Acton, "Power corrupts: absolute power corrupts absolutely."

Societies tend to follow the thesis of Ray Dalio, founder of Bridgewater Associates, who expressed an archetypical cycle in his bestselling book *The Changing World Order*:

THE RISE:

1. Strong leadership
2. Inventiveness
3. Education
4. Strong culture
5. Good resource allocation
6. Good competitiveness
7. Strong income growth
8. Strong markets and financial centers

THE ZENITH:

1. Less productivity
2. Overextension
3. Losing competitiveness
4. Wealth gaps

THE DECLINE:

1. Large debts
2. Printing money
3. Internal conflict
4. Loss of reserve currency status (Holland, Great Britain, United States?)
5. Weak leadership
6. Civil war / revolution

This summary perspective is the result of fifty years of research by Ray Dalio and his corporate team of researchers. Their rigorous analysis of data worldwide covered centuries and millennia and included interviews and discussions with the most involved, respected, and recognized leaders of many disciplines over time.

There are three main cycles that occur repeatedly and require constant vigilance:

1. The long-term debt and capital markets cycle

2. The internal order and disorder cycle

3. The external order and disorder cycle

These cycles swing back and forth between peace and war, economic boom and bust, transitions of power between the political left and right, and the coalescence and disintegration of empires. Embedded in the swings in one direction are the ingredients that lead to the swings in the opposite direction.

There are many other determinants that influence the timing, extent, magnitude, and impact of the confluence of these cycles, like geography, geology, acts of nature, governmental/rule of law upheavals, and the wealth gap narrowing or widening. All these factors are important in deciphering where a society is on this continuum.

It is then that we can begin to see the impact of Critical Thinking and the need for Education to uncover these swings so that our society can make effective course corrections. In making these corrections, we prevent mistakes in action and effort to overcome the slide to anarchy and, ultimately, annihilation.

After all, at the end of the day, humankind has survived. At present, most of us have been employed, have shelter, make money, and have managed to outrun plagues and epidemics. We, as a collective body, have endured together. Will we eliminate pain and pestilence, war and poverty, famine and genocide, and brutality visited upon the weak and unprepared? No. But if we can recognize the facts as they are, we can mitigate and defuse the worst consequences of these patterns and cycles.

DEMOCRACY AND THE AMERICAN CONSTITUTIONAL REPUBLIC

A true democracy is merely government by plurality, while a constitutional republic (i.e., the United States) adds other safeguards to prevent the "tyranny of the majority." Our Founding Fathers showed incredible foresight in the design of the institutions and mechanisms they built into our Constitution. Further improvements have been made through the Amendments, which have further strengthened our governmental institutions.

One critical distinction of this constitutional republic is the electoral college. Though highly debated today, Critical Thinking is employed and helps us to prevent pure democracy with its potential for tyranny by the majority. The electoral college mechanism enhances the voting power of individual states and prevents popular national movements from simply drowning out their voices. The current "winner takes all" format keeps the voice of each state relatively strong, so that all states have a stake in national elections.

In writing the Declaration of Independence, the Articles of Confederation, the Constitution, and the associated Bill of Rights, the Founding Fathers granted a safeguard to oppose the erosion of society. (See also appendix 6b.) They wisely included the Tenth Amendment to ensure that "the powers not delegated to the United States by the Constitution, nor prohibited by it to the States, are reserved to the States respectively, or to the people." This limiting term was meant to restrain the growth of the federal government by regulating its responsibilities and setting limits on those powers.

Thus, if the United States of America is to remain a beacon of freedom to the world, it must fight against the ever-present desire of the bureaucratic state to co-opt the legislative bodies to increase their power and control over the citizenry. (See also appendix 1e.) After all, the purpose of the government is to serve its citizens, not the other way around. The goal, therefore, should be to refine in perpetuity the streamlining of government through its laws and regulations. This process allows for the most efficient administration of governmental activity while giving the citizens the freest and unencumbered environment to pursue their self-interests.

BUREAUCRATIC AND REGULATORY CREEP

If a country's governance is to truly be "of the people, by the people, for the people," elected officials must answer "to the people." Answering to the people requires that laws, rules, and regulations be established with the approval of the elected representatives. If this process is followed properly, then bureaucrats should only be allowed to give input toward the creation of new regulations, not to create them without oversight and approval from the elected representatives.

In addition, any regulations should be succinct and clearly stated so that people can easily understand them. For example, Hammurabi's legal code was etched into a single pillar for anyone to see. Israelites were expected to have memorized their law, and some even managed to fit it into their hats. When the rules were focused, civilizations thrived culturally. Crime went down, and more people were able to avoid breaking laws and support law enforcement.

The purpose of regulations is to make sure that society is not abused. To that end, some regulations could be designed with sunset provisions that would require future representative approval for their continuation. Thus, regulations would not arbitrarily remain on the books and active. All others should be eliminated to make the regulated state as streamlined as possible.

Regulation clarity and simplicity are extremely important. Too often, regulations have been written by so-called experts, whose very purpose is to create complexity, enhancing the individual author's acclaim to the detriment of the regulation. The purpose is usually to increase the value of the author's expertise, which helps them to land lucrative private sector jobs.

It is unfortunate, but History shows that government and, therefore, bureaucratic growth often become a purpose unto itself. This is why the focus should always be on limiting the size of government and keeping the government focused on its primary responsibility to serve the citizens. However, our country seems to be taking steps back toward this simplicity, with authority being turned back over to the voting citizens with a stunning Supreme Court ruling.

In early July 2024, the Supreme Court overruled the Chevron Doctrine that came from the Supreme Court's 1984 decision in *Chevron v. Natural Resources Defense Council*. That decision in 1984 basically stated that if federal legislation is ambiguous or leaves an administrative gap, the courts must defer to the regulatory agency's interpretation if the interpretation is reasonable. That empowered the regulators to be author, judge, and jury with regard to the application of regulations. This case stole away the courts' responsibility to interpret the plain meaning of the laws that were passed and gave that power to those writing the regulations and the regulators themselves. The Supreme Court, on behalf of the American people, disagreed with this effort.

In a constitutional republic, the people should have the final say on what stays or goes. But this decision robbed them of the appropriate congressional oversight. The court in 2024 helped reestablish the checks and balances and reduced the power of the bureaucratic state, which had previously answered to no one.

A government's responsibility is to lay the groundwork for an optimal environment that allows the individual to pursue their happiness. The only constraint is that the individual must not abuse or infringe upon the rights of others as they live their lives. Within our founding documents, the concept of power seemingly flows from the integrity, honesty, accountability, and virtue of our elected representatives. This protection provides the foundation for economic advancement and the coordination of all aspects of the government for the good of our citizens. Without that integrity, we lose the government's ability to protect the individual.

This raises the issue of power—the ability to enforce one's will on others. Inevitably, power drifts, wanders, and morphs into control, the imposition of will, and megalomania. The fewer checks and balances, the more likely a division of government will abuse its control. We would do well to consider the words of Benjamin Franklin when asked if America was to be a monarchy or a republic: "A republic, if you can keep it!"

POWER OF THE US MILITARY

The power to raise a military and employ it on behalf of the people comes from the constitution. The military was created and is sustained under the operation of the civilian government. While it takes direction from the president, only Congress has the power to declare war.

Many presidents in the United States have worked around that limitation and employed the military without Congress's consent to a declaration of war. There is a lot of gray area in doing that. Protecting the country's self-interests and keeping threats further from our shores are some grounds that presidents have invoked when skirting Congress. The election process provides a convincing resolution to the attempt to ignore the power of the people.

POWER OF THE GOVERNMENT

The government derives its just powers from the consent of the governed. The government serves the citizenry, not the other way around. As life has advanced over the last century, our society has become more complex. There are many conflicting interests the US government must navigate in the pursuit of providing the optimal existence for the citizenry while also protecting it from bad consequences—militarily, economically, and environmentally.

As John Trenchard and Thomas Gordon, authors of the 1723 *Cato's Letters*, wrote, there must be accountability within the law. There is the law of equity (to not harm one another) and the law of self-preservation (to defend oneself). We must, therefore, have accountability between these two needs. Add to this the principle that "absolute power corrupts absolutely," and we quickly see the need for accountability.

Just as Cato warned in Rome, and as Ray Dalio continues to warn, the life cycle of empires holds a desire for coddling and indulgence, born out of previous toil and strength, until one grows tired of such effort and decline continues apace.

So how does this complex environment of government, military, and economic activities impact our ability to "keep" a republic?

The answer is simple.

We all have opinions. As we should. But we should strive to build our opinions on accurate information. With all the talk about disinformation, misinformation, and falsehoods, in addition to the rise of the internet, it is clear as to the need for Critical Thinking. The reporting of news today is more often opinion, and biased opinion, instead of fact—logical, intelligent, and documented fact.

Sophocles once said, "What people believe prevails over the truth." For this reason, humanity *must* question everything. The need for Critical Thinking has never been greater.

Critical Thinking gives us the ability to overcome disinformation; therefore, censorship needs to be outlawed. Censorship is the enemy of free speech, and freedom of speech is fundamental to well-formed opinions. Within the operation of government, there must be mechanisms for the citizenry to question, identify, and propose solutions to those mechanisms that don't serve the citizens properly. The act of censoring does not allow information, correct or incorrect, to flow freely. Without that free flow, Critical Thinking can not be applied to the end of improving the government mechanisms.

There are often powerful forces attempting to alter the balance of power within the government. These forces may seek to hijack the narrative. These attempts to appropriate the narrative require our utmost diligence. As in science, one cannot prove things to be absolutely correct. But you can test theories and hypothesize whether the attempt to control the narrative is in the interest of the citizens or whether such efforts are to be at the expense of the citizens. Critical Thinking is required to identify whether the levers of government are being well applied or if individuals are seeking to manipulate organizations and/or mechanisms to the citizens' detriment. Understanding the various forms of government that have appeared throughout History, gives every citizen a massive advantage over those seeking to hijack their society.

Any form of government is in danger of falling into certain typical shortfalls. One of the simplest ways to prevent bureaucratic erosion in our republic is by maintaining accountability and transparency.

Keep the government small and focused on its mission. When politicians create the system and then feed on the system, they create and impose a significant conflict of interest on the country. And thus they begin eroding the fabric of society's strength upon which society is fundamentally dependent.

Career politicians can become the leeches of a democratic state. Critical Thinking, a review of History, accountability, and transparency will create an improved environment, allowing us to find better solutions to the issues we are confronted with. Perhaps the term limit is an important answer that can contribute to solving numerous problems being faced. Perhaps better incentives or cutting funding. In any case, the fewer players there are to hold accountable, the fewer problems are likely to arise. The electorate needs to realize that less government is key to achieving successful government oversight. After all, the less you have to oversee, the more proficiently you can fulfill that task. The acronym KISS (Keep It Simple, Stupid) would seem to apply quite effectively here.

As stated, there are numerous forms of government from which to choose, assuming they participate in a representative government. The sad reality is that when Critical Thinking is not applied and the citizens vote their representatives into office, they may find that their decision has placed the power of the government in the hands of those who would eliminate the citizens' rights and become a totalitarian state. We've seen this happen in Venezuela (Chavez and Maduro). Or the revolutionaries themselves may just take control of the state as a result of the revolution's outcome, such as what happened in Cuba (Fidel Castro), China (Mao), Russia (Stalin)—the list from history goes on.

Once a representative government has been hijacked, it may not be possible to get back to a representative form of government. That is why the citizens' right to vote is such an important obligation. The integrity of the voting process is likewise key to the ongoing success of a representative government. Our Founding Fathers would have met the executioner had the American Revolution failed. They could not have committed a greater potential sacrifice. The concluding sentence of the Declaration of Independence reads, "[W]e mutually pledge to each other our Lives, our Fortunes, and our Sacred Honor." Unlike other leaders in History, our Founding Fathers were truly altruists, not seeking selfish gains but rather dedicated to the improvement of the lives of the citizens of their new country. Using Critical Thinking, their Education, their Religious Values, and their knowledge of History's successes and failures, they proposed "a more perfect union."

But can we save it?

GOVERNMENT-RELATED HISTORICAL QUOTES

"The Goal of Socialism is Communism."

(Vladimir Lenin)

"Only a virtuous people are capable of freedom. As nations become corrupt and vicious, they have more need of masters."

(Benjamin Franklin)

"Fascism and Communism are not two opposites, but two rival gangs fighting over the same territory—both are variants of statism, based on the collectivist principle that man is the rightless slave of the state."

(Ayn Rand)

"There is no difference between Communism and Socialism, except in the means of achieving the same ultimate end: Communism proposes to enslave men by force, Socialism—by vote. It is merely the difference between murder and suicide."

(Ayn Rand)

"Most people who read 'The Communist Manifesto' probably have no idea that it was written by a couple of young men who had never worked a day in their lives, and who nevertheless spoke boldly in the name of 'the workers.'"

(Thomas Sowell)

"Those who want to reap the benefits of this great nation (The United States) must bear the fatigue of supporting it."

(THOMAS PAINE)

"Violence is not necessary to destroy a civilization. Each civilization dies from indifference toward the unique Values which created it."

(NICOLAS GOMEZ DAVILA)

"The world will not be destroyed by those who do evil, but by those who watch them without doing anything."

(ALBERT EINSTEIN)

"If you do not take an interest in the affairs of your government, then you are doomed to live under the rule of fools." (Plato)

"Those who deny freedom to others. Deserve it not for themselves."

(ABRAHAM LINCOLN)

"When the Government fears the people, there is liberty. When the people fear the government, there is tyranny."

(THOMAS JEFFERSON)

"Government should govern for the good of the people, not for the good of those in power."

(ARISTOTLE)

For more on Political Systems, see appendix 5.

CHAPTER 6
ECONOMIC SYSTEMS

The Economic System serves at the convenience of its respective Political System. This bedrock principle is essential for any society to understand. While thePolitical System is the final arbiter of behavior within the Economic System, people live their lives within the Economic System. The Economic System is where we contribute our labor, intellect, and efforts toward the ongoing operation and development of the national economy while pursuing our own self-interests.

Therefore, it is imperative for the survival of any Political System that it prioritize the establishment of a favorable and efficient Economic System. Four Economic Systems have dominated the past century, as governments attempt to keep up with the industrialization of the world:

1. *Communism* is where the government owns and controls all property. By doing so, they control the levers of the economy and the people by proxy.

2. *Socialism* has various levels of private ownership with heavy government oversight, which in some cases tends toward communism. The government controls industry in the belief that government decisions are superior to corporate decisions. It aims to evenly distribute resources, goods, and services to everyone with the goal of ensuring equality.

3. *Fascism* allows for private ownership, but corporations must support the government or lose control of their business. This system is usually associated with a dictatorship and the effective control of all portions of the economy.

Note that these first three Economic Systems often occur under totalitarian governments, where risk tolerance and Critical Thinking are discouraged.

4. *Capitalism,* on the other hand, is an economy of private corporations and free markets where decisions are made freely by the citizens. They engage in the competitive process of price point discovery in the free market, which has the effect of finding the most reasonable value in the pricing structure of a competitive marketplace while encouraging business. Here, we find risk tolerance and Critical Thinking are highly valued.

If we believe the best Economic System is that which allows the creativity of individuals to address opportunities with the greatest freedom, free of fear of overbearing oversight, then neither communism, socialism, or fascism could be considered optimal. Therefore, the question is where and how capitalism can best function and thrive.

Winston Churchill famously said, "Democracy is the worst form of government except for all those others that have been tried from time to time." The same could be said about capitalism. In a capitalist country, citizens, not governments, own and run companies. These companies compete with other companies for business. They decide which goods and services to provide, the price of those goods and services, and how to sell them. Business owners employ workers who have volunteered their labor for the compensation offered. Labor does not own the means of production.

Capitalism is the only Economic System that can optimally harness the power of the individual's pursuit of self-interest while meeting the demands of the marketplace. Price point discovery is an economic process to establish value for products and services. It provides market equilibrium between supply and demand in the marketplace. In other words, variable supply and demand govern economic strength and weakness over time.

Totalitarian states are states in which the government controls the governed. There has never been a centrally planned economy that has managed to harness the individual's pursuit of self-interest while also encouraging that individual to make positive contributions to society. Democratic freedom allows individuals to think, act, reflect, live, present, challenge, reasonably protest, vote, and generally express viewpoints without fear of retribution, which, along with free markets, allows humankind's creativity and development to flourish. Markets develop to meet those wants and needs. New markets create new industries, jobs, income, and growth. Those who deny these freedoms do not see fruitful results. It's very straightforward.

Any Political System must advocate for a legal structure to maintain, support, and enforce the rules and requirements of society for it to thrive. Capitalism is no different. Without advocacy for the benefit of its citizens, Political Systems can hijack the Economic System. And that advocacy requires the citizenry to Think Critically, Question often, and Speak their minds to preclude the creation of a hijacked system.

In today's culture, capitalism is often disparaged; however, in the free marketplace, competition spawns human creativity and progress as people seek the opportunity to produce better value for the purchaser. The purpose of both Economic and Political Systems is to achieve full employment, but—and this is key—you can't continually employ individuals without profit. The search for and attainment of profit is the engine that continues to employ the free market populace. Profit is the fuel that allows the majority of citizens to remain productively employed by the economy's engine and the individual companies in particular.

The marketplace can be brutal, but it is efficient. In the end, if we don't allow markets to run their natural course, societal chaos and collapse can occur when the natural forces of markets get overtaken by government dictates. Those dictates are intended for indoctrination instead of supporting the Critical Thinking process that allows free markets to flourish.

Totalitarian regimes survive on power, often brutally applied, along with what may be temporary societal success. Fascism, socialism, and communism all claim to put societal success over the individual. But they forget that we all have a natural sense of self-preservation. Their elites continue to seek their own interests despite advising the citizens to the contrary.

As Charlie Munger (vice chairman of Berkshire Hathaway) pointed out, if a segment of society refuses to work but continues to receive economic benefits for free from the rest of society, the capitalist structure will be disrupted and ultimately put at risk. Munger is famous for stating that he would rather deal with inequality in life for some, and a functioning capitalist system for many, than poverty for all.

C. S. Lewis also pointed out, "Of all tyrannies a tyranny sincerely exercised for the good of its victims may be the most oppressive." Totalitarian regimes try to dumb things down by removing freedom in the marketplace. In short, totalitarian regimes in their effort to control, remove human creativity from the market process.

In 1776, Adam Smith described the free market system. His thesis was and remains simple: Allowing people to focus on their own self-interest produces economic benefits that can be shared by all the country's citizens. This was directly and indirectly included in the drafting of the US Constitution in 1787 and the attendant Bill of Rights in 1791. This was not an original American thought however. As early as the thirteenth century, the philosopher St. Thomas Aquinas worked to explain the full range of human actions and social organizations. His followers maintained his vision and observed the existence of economic law and how inexorable forces of cause and effect operate as any other natural law.

Economic law explains the principles of supply and demand, the causes of inflation, the operation of foreign exchange rates, and a general understanding of economic value. In the past eight centuries, the world of economics has exploded with the fruit of human labor. We now take for granted the economic discoveries of past centuries, which today we call Common Sense. This includes seeing the market as an entrepreneurial exercise requiring a medium of exchange (money) and seeing the nature of individual choices and preferences.

In the early twentieth century, Austrian economist John Schumpeter began to decipher business cycles and how capitalistic economies develop. Schumpeter's major thesis concluded that entrepreneurship was the cornerstone of capitalism, the source of innovation vital to driving the economy. He identified five key areas where entrepreneurship could drive development:

1. A new good
2. A new method of production
3. A new market
4. A new source of supply
5. A new organization of an industry

Schumpeter's term *creative destruction* was the process of industrial mutation continuously revolutionizing the economic structure from within, incessantly destroying the old one, and resulting in the new economic structure being in a perpetual state of change and recreation while adding efficiency and value.

With the global outbreak of socialism and communism in the nineteenth century, the development of economic theory fell under attack by the combined forces of politics (the proletariat) and weak governments.

Socialism is a political and economic theory of social organization advocating for government ownership and/or regulation of the means of production, distribution, and subsequent exchange. It presumes that its leadership by the few elites know what is best for the many individuals. Do the citizens vote for politicians so that the politicians can dictate to the citizenry? We think not. Have we not noticed that the government has taken hold of the sovereignty principle and is now administering all decisions? The sovereignty of a nation is for the benefit of its citizens, not the government.

Looking at daily economic and political issues, governments often peer through the unfocused lens of current needs and wants and miss the long-term consequences of their actions. This shortsightedness invariably leads to excesses, corruption, and the ultimate downfall of the very system that was intended to protect. Critical Thinking is a vital protection from such excesses, corruption, and downfall.

Machiavelli and others denied the existence of objective truth and posited that everything is malleable. If something does not seem good, and you want to do it, then you should do it and call it good. If something causes you pain, it can be fixed. If one works hard enough, one can determine the outcomes.

The central question of "What is good?" has morphed instead into "How do you get it done?" And when asked what *it* is, the answer is, "Whatever you want it to be."

Then economic and political changes began to spiral out of control at roughly the same time as did social programs, social equity, and handouts. We can readily agree that the enactment of socialism would result in utter chaos and the end of civilization (in accordance with Mises and Hayek of the Austrian School of Economics).

In addition to others, Friedrich Hayek also warned of the dangers of credit expansion, with the biggest risk being a currency crisis. In Hayek, one can see the direct opposition to John Maynard Keynes and the use of exchange rates, government intervention in the capital markets, as well as Keynes's analysis of the pros and cons of monetary reform (ee *Road to Serfdom by* Hayek).

From Keynes's perspective, we can see the introduction of modern monetary theory, which posits that there can never be too much debt as long as society is provided the liquidity for economic function and political justice. Yet people often forget that Keynes called to reduce the debt when the economy had recovered. Politicians don't like to talk about that part.

As a result of this misinterpretation, many presumed that debt no longer mattered. In fact, Economic Nobel Laureate Paul Krugman and Stephanie Kelton have proposed the creation of single commodity coins, which are proudly proclaimed to be worth $1 trillion, and the releasing of these coins into the Treasury to balance the budgets, saying, "Debt is money we owe to ourselves" (Krugman, *Forbes Magazine*, February 17, 2015). This thinking says that, as long as we pay the market interest rate to ourselves, the rest of the massive debt is of no consequence.

We do have a major problem with the intersectionality of societies, Economic Systems, political structures, and the individuals they are all bound to honor and protect. When the needs of the community surpass the normal, natural replenishment ability of the community, the allocation of resources can become based upon need (instead of earned allotment). When the proletariats demand creates a loss of equilibrium, the entire society and the propulsion of its future are in jeopardy. Too much demand chasing too little supply; too much spending versus too little revenue—these imbalances lead to currency valuation problems, the eventual debasement of currency, inflation (if not hyperinflation), and eventually, the economic ruin of the society.

Modern monetary theory supposes that, for the first time in History, governments do not rely on taxes or borrowing for spending. This is largely because today they can print as much money as they need and are the monopoly issuers of their currency (the United States, the United Kingdom, Japan, and Canada). After all, as the alleged experts say, "We owe the debt to ourselves."

In the esteemed words of Margaret Thatcher, "The problem with socialism is that you eventually run out of other people's money."

The same can be said for the lending and borrowing of most major players on the world stage today. Imagine balancing your personal budget and expenses. Now imagine you heard online that debt is an illusion, and if you pretend it doesn't exist, it can't hurt you. You max out your credit cards, empty your bank account, and take out exorbitant loans. It appears you are living large until your debtors come to collect. Then, suddenly, you learn just how heavy the weight of debt really can be.

We believe strongly that the laws of economics and economic exchange require equilibrium to avoid an inflationary spiral. Any society with a functioning economy requires Faith and trust in the currency to define what it is worth. Once the integrity of currency is lost and the buying power of a currency disintegrates, you find that no amount of growth and productivity gain can compensate for the loss of value. Like the Weimar Republic, eventually, you will have so much money printed with a value approaching zero that it will take wheelbarrows of the stuff to buy a loaf of bread. Today we see a similar path before our homelands as we come to the intersection of politics and economics. We desperately need the application of Critical Thinking to the forces of economic, political, and social change occurring around us.

When we take an inventory of the many aspects of politics that depend on a solid economy, it can cause real concern about the shape of our nation. Think about it. Elections, infrastructure, Education, safety (both internal police powers and national defense), commerce and trade, and even promoting the health of the citizenry all need to be funded. Without a sustainable Economic System, none of these fundamental pieces can function.

And what can preserve the ongoing efforts to deliver a government of, by, and for the people? Democracy offers a solution (and a democratic republic an even better solution). It incorporates the will of the individual with the narrow but real needs of a government structure. This makes the consent of the governed vital.

The presumption that the government, by its very existence, becomes the will of the people and knows best for all is abhorrent. This is the soft-spoken word whispered to inform someone they are no longer their own. This elitist attitude towards the governed eventually leads to chaos, rebellion, and anarchy. Ultimately, totalitarianism fills the vacuum.

The government that owns and controls all aspects of civilian life may hijack and destroy its ability to flourish. An Economic System serves at the convenience of the Political System. It is critical to understand that one cannot talk about how to design and optimize an Economic System without understanding the governmental system or structure it must function within.

The best government system is the one that provides the infrastructure and competitive protections for the optimal production of the services and goods its citizenry demands and allows for freedom of thought. If there is economic growth for the individual, then there is economic growth for the country. The largest problems for any economy arise when the government attempts to do too much for too many using artificial levers. The infrastructure and competitive protections are not limitless. As economies surge, cumbersome laws and regulations can present their own problems and sabotage all that was good in the economic progress being made. The least restrictive, while still being a sensible form of government, is a democratic republic.

Capitalism naturally encompasses vital concepts, such as the need for the following:

1. A drafted, written, and adopted rule of law
2. Education with honest, consistent, and transparent protocols
3. Critical Thinking
4. Common Sense
5. Freedom of Speech
6. Protection from out-of-control political structures and forces
7. Harnessing the power of the pursuit of self-interest
8. Price point discovery, competition, curiosity, and creativity contributing to the optimization of the capitalist system.

Even when understanding the fundamental principle that the Economic System serves at the convenience of the Political System, the citizenry can still vote for politicians who become dictators in office. This would be a tragedy because capitalism is where market forces, innovation, and competition are allowed to work their magic. It is capitalism that has been the greatest conduit in History through which humanity's long-term economic success has soared. It is not that the economic results will be perfect in capitalism. Rather, it is what some call "the law of large numbers" at work. The largest number of citizens will benefit under capitalism, as opposed to the tyranny that results under any of the various forms of collectivism (totalitarianism).

We believe a capitalistic system under the constitutional republic offers an optimal combination of specific Political and Economic

Systems. If we truly value human independence and freedom along with the basic protections of their society, we must select that combination to produce the freedom people should possess. We must also realize (as pointed out at different points of this book) that there will always be dangers to deal with and developments that man hasn't seen yet. To combat these dangers, we must always be ready to apply our Critical Thinking.

> *The inherent vice of capitalism is the unequal sharing of blessings; the inherent virtue of socialism is the equal sharing of miseries.*
>
> (WINSTON CHURCHILL)

> *Human beings are born with different capacities. If they are free, they are not equal. And if they are equal, they are not free.*
>
> (ALEKSANDR SOLZHENITSYN)

> *When you see that in order to produce, you need to obtain permission from men who produce nothing—when you see that money is flowing to those who deal, not in goods, but in favors—when you see that men get richer by graft and by pull than by work, and your laws don't protect you against them, but protect them against you—when you see corruption being rewarded and honesty becoming a self-sacrifice—You may know that your society is doomed.*
>
> (AYN RAND, ATLAS SHRUGGED, 1957)

CONCLUDING THOUGHTS

It was with great trepidation that we set out to write this collection of essays.

It is our hope that we have succeeded in our attempt to resurrect basic eternal truths, champion rational and Critical Thought, recover historical insights, and demonstrate that Critical Thinking, like a tapestry, must be woven into our educational, religious, historical, political, and economic structures. Let us begin again to think for ourselves, draw our own conclusions in our journey toward humanity's continuous evolution, and march toward progress. Let us take back what it really means to be *progressive*—a term that should reflect thoughts and actions for the true and real benefit of all humanity throughout the world.

Concerned with daily events and the movements of the early twenty-first century—many of which came to fruition through shallow, if not ignorant, groupthink—we felt an intense need to wipe the slate clean and lay out certain fundamentals of Critical Thought to mitigate and combat the hijacking of logic, rational thought, and belief in eternal truths.

Everywhere we looked, we saw basic human truths corrupted for emotional, intellectual, and financial gain at the expense of society. The facts were suddenly irrelevant. The Common Sense of what is right and wrong was thrown out. Freedoms to Think, Question, and Speak critically were being eroded.

And this continues today. People talk past each other while engaging with social media technology that precludes real face-to-face human contact. It is not surprising to see people walk into each other or walk into doors or buildings while engrossed with the latest nonsense on their phones.

Our intended audience is anyone sensing there is something amiss—with the way we engage, with the regression of thought, with the desire for truth, and with the increasingly disparate and polarized perspectives. We wanted to engage those who would find Ayn Rand's *Atlas Shrugged*, Aldous Huxley's *Brave New World*, or George Orwell's *1984* to be prophetic. We wanted to help those who wanted to help themselves as they look forward and care for the future, for themselves, for their lives and rights, for their families, for their communities, for their livelihoods, and for their country.

We care deeply about these things. We also understand how fragile the march of humankind can be. One can plainly see the wrong turns that can be taken by society and the detrimental impacts such turns can have. These can lead to chaos or worse, as revealed by our overview of the History of civilization. But perhaps there are a few ideas, a few common-sense understandings, and some Critical Thinking that can help to stem this tide of self-destruction.

Critical Thinking requires reasoned, logical, coherent, and concise conclusions, which are essential to understanding the ramifications of indoctrination. It (Critical Thinking) does not simply accept all arguments and judgments, but rather questions and inquires in an effort to find fundamental truth. Indeed, Critical Thinkers are skeptical and open-minded. They value fair-mindedness, respect evidence and reasoning, and appreciate clarity and precision. They look at different points of view and will change positions when reason leads them to do so.

Such Critical Thought is vital to appreciate, embrace, and understand the impact upon the foundational topics we set out to examine:

1. Critical Thinking: Definition and Application
2. Education
3. Religion, Faith, and Values
4. History
5. Political Systems
6. Economic Systems

The application of Critical Thinking is enabled through Education, but it is informed by Religion, Faith, and the Values they create. Our Founding Fathers were religious. Everything they did in founding our Republic was well informed by their Religion, Faith, and resulting Values. We believe a republic's government should be of the people, by the people, and for the people. Therefore, the employees and the politicians of the government are employees of the people and consequently, public servants of the people, not masters of the people. The resulting bureaucracy of regulators is not to be a fourth branch of government.

Intelligence misapplied is a very dangerous thing. Without great Values, actions of this type can have a very detrimental impact on the fabric of society and, therefore, the progress of that society.

And so, in our conclusion, we would be remiss not to review what historical societies have experienced from their rise to their fall. As we cited Alexander Tytler's "Cycle of Freedom" in an earlier chapter, we must be ever vigilant to prove him wrong, that it simply cannot exist as a permanent form of government. (See appendix 6c for a fuller treatment of Tytler's Cycle and additional commentary.)

What this book has covered is the logical development of humanity, its tools for progress, including the application of Critical Thinking protocols and regimens; the inputs of Education, Religion and Values; History; Political Systems; and Economic Systems. Those, along with the application of Critical Thinking, have gotten us to where we are today. But where will the future take us?

Tytler's "Cycle of Freedom" is a harbinger of decline unless overcome through the application of Critical Thinking.

Humanity is always in the pursuit of the meaning of their individual lives. While that is a constant, the chapters of this book may help those who are in this search. Meaning goes beyond oneself and is truly found in each individual's dedication to their value system (discovered most easily in their Religion), their family, their community, their nation, and even globally for some.

However, the tools of understanding and analysis presented here may not be enough to deal with beyond the present. That is because humankind is about to be overtaken by a technology that humanity doesn't have the historical experience to properly control. Artificial intelligence (AI), artificial general intelligence (AGI, intelligence equal to a human), and artificial super intelligence (ASI, intelligence greater than *any* human) are stages of technological development that are here or about to be here.

As such, we must recognize the search for incontrovertible, irrefutable, and foundational truth—not algorithm-controlled "truth." The transparency supplied with absolute truth properly encouraged and regulated will act as the most powerful tool in assisting humanity to digest the massive changes that continuously and almost overwhelmingly introduce themselves to our lives.

The one thing that has been a constant is ever-accelerating change. While humanity has historically responded in different ways over the centuries and millennia to change, change has made itself known and incorporated itself into our daily lives.

AI, along with robotics and the various applications of blockchain technology, is about to accelerate change to an even more rapid pace. These forces are too powerful to be denied; therefore, they must be embraced, their benefits implemented, and their detrimental forces controlled and regulated for the benefit of society.

As Jeff Brown of Brownstone Research said (on February 17, 2025 in his publication "The Bleeding Edge"), "Competition and truth will weed out the foundation (AI) models that are trying to manipulate us." We would highlight the huge contribution that transparency must add to make that reality come true.

The tools within the human brain are those we have always had. The key is Critical Thinking. The environment is changing rapidly. AI, robotics, and blockchain offer many positive opportunities but also many detrimental and sometimes scary possibilities. Add the following sentence: The Large Language Models (LLMs) which train AI software need to be taught with emphasis on the contents of this book, specifically Religion, Faith, and Values, to prevent AI from becoming an abusive force. The objective is to focus on eternal / absolute truth.

Capitalism is not perfect. To paraphrase what Churchill's longer quote said about democracy, "It is the worst system except for all the rest." It is the one system that can harness the power of the individual's pursuit of self-interest. The competitive forces in price point discovery are the engine behind employing citizens of each nation to contribute their efforts in exchange for compensation. The marketplace is a tough place. Competitive forces are tough forces. People must adapt to the ever-increasing pace of change to remain competitive in their field and employable in general. What has been described is complex, demanding, and hard. It is the only Economic System in which all people, if they so choose, can freely participate.

If one believes, as the authors do, that the United States is the last, best example of capitalism at work within our constitutional republic (even with all its shortcomings) then we, as a nation, must be diligent and continuous in our support for a government of the people, by the people, and for the people. To quote Ronald Reagan:

> Freedom is never more than one generation away from extinction. We didn't pass it on to our children in the bloodstream. The only way they can inherit the freedom we have known is if we fight for it, protect it, defend it, and then hand it to them with the well-fought lessons of how they, in their lifetime, must do the same. And if you and I don't do this, then you and I may well spend our sunset years telling our children and our children's children what it once was like in America when men were free. (1961)

Critical Thinking permeates our study and exposition of Education; Religion, Faith, and Values; History; Political Systems; and Economic Systems. Without Critical Thinking applied to all aspects of our lives and our country, we face our future with serious uncertainty and dangerous consequences. The environment is changing rapidly.

Therefore, from the introduction to this concluding section, the question is, Can we save our republic from being hijacked?

That is for you to answer through your own participation and use of Critical Thinking in the Political and Economic System while being informed by Education; Religion, Faith, and Values; and History.

We wish you encouragement as you persevere toward rediscovering humankind and helping in its pursuit of progress and the truth.

> *We've been conditioned to think that only politicians can solve our problems. But at some point, maybe we will wake up and recognize that it was the politicians who created our problems.*
>
> (Dr. Ben Carson)

> *No Society ever thrives because it has a large and growing class of parasites living off those who produce.*
>
> (Thomas Sowell)

> *It is the peculiar quality of a fool to perceive the faults of others and to forget his own.*
>
> (Cicero)

APPENDICES

The following appendices expand on concepts established in the previous chapters. They are numbered based on the chapter they reference (1–6) and the order they appear in that chapter (a,b,c, etc.). The first number shows what chapter it relates to, and the second character is a letter that helps distinguish the different appendices that apply to a chapter. Due to the interrelatedness of the chapters, some appendices may be referred to in a chapter but numbered as relating more dominantly to another chapter.

APPENDIX 1A: CRITICAL TERMS AND CONCEPTS TO BE APPLIED IN CRITICAL THINKING

If you commit to your position before the mutual exchange of information, you may be committing yourself to being wrong. It is more helpful to find a phrase when introducing your information from which you draw your conclusion, like, "I could be wrong, but . . ."

Using this phrase or another of your own invention allows you to indicate you have an open mind to new information. It also avoids a strong, belligerent opening, which may cause the individual significant embarrassment when conclusion-changing information is introduced. By using open-minded phraseology, the individual prepares to express their logic from their critical thinking on the topic. But also they indicate their open-mindedness to allow true critical thinking to occur rather than committing to their initial conclusion, which may be in error.

Thus, the definitions for terms and phrases that follow will help the reader look deeper and pursue the process of thinking more critically.

Brainstorming and Collaboration

Brainstorming is the art of getting a group of people together to throw out unfiltered ideas to work toward improvements or solutions to problems. It is a creative process. It takes a unique set of characteristics to create a truly collaborative and effective brainstorming environment. You are asking participants to throw out their immediate, reactive ideas without filtering them and protecting themselves from ridicule and negative reactions. They are exposing themselves by offering spontaneous ideas. As such, they should not be held accountable for their ideas. It is meant to be a positive process, where ideas that are believed to be constructively helpful are responded to in a positive manner.

Negativity kills spontaneity. Spontaneity is vital for brainstorming sessions. Without it, people will not return to participate effectively.

Brainstorming is a creative process that tries to compress time to work toward improvements and answers that are the purpose of the meeting. To be successful, the tone can only be positive, with no humor at the expense of participants—including communication after the meeting. This is difficult to do when you understand human nature universally.

If we look for the fabric of our society to strengthen, then we need to positively participate in creating and reinforcing those rules, standards, morals, ethics, institutions, and laws—and, as such, their dependability, their consistency, their open and free competitive environments, and the freedom of thought, questioning, and speech as the bedrock of all other freedoms, from which creativity springs.

Curiosity and creativity

Curiosity is what leads to creativity. *Webster's Dictionary* defines *creativity* as "an original product of human intellectual invention." These are creative thoughts. Whether these visions are an answer to a problem, a dream, or a desire, humans are always looking to overcome obstacles. Doesn't the history of humankind demonstrate the incredible inventiveness of the human mind over and over again?

Whether it takes the form of medical solutions, technological advancements, or embracing the laws of physics (like aviation or sending rockets to space), humans are always looking for solutions. But are these not solutions to perceived problems? Some so-called problems may be obvious. But all too often, when we are looking to solve *something*, we may be attempting to solve a **symptom** and not the actual **problem**.

So the first step in the human creative attempt to solve *something* is to accurately define the actual problem. The phrase to always apply is, Have you identified a **symptom** or the **true problem** before creating a solution?

Creativity, or creative vision for that matter, requires the ability to think and communicate freely. If the ability to think and communicate freely is **controlled** in any fashion, it is our belief that the inhibiting impact of that **control** will result in the reduction of free inquiry and, as such, greatly impede humankind's creativity and progress. It is an open inquiry into all fields of endeavor that allows the realization of the fruits of such creativity.

Competition

Freedom of thought, questioning, and speech is fundamental to the creativity of humankind. With these freedoms maintained, many alternative ideas will arise and thrive. To have an impact, a creative proposal must reach some form of **critical mass** that creates a momentum of interest and demand. It is in all the myriad of **idea marketplaces** that humankind weeds out its priorities, helping society make decisions on how to apply resources in order to begin making progress on the chosen ideas. The rise of competition in virtually every marketplace helps humankind realize consistent, rapid improvements in those same markets.

Example: Think of the choice of cars manufactured under Stalin's communism in the post–World War II era versus those that were rapidly developing under US automobile manufacturers at the same time. Comparing manufacturing in the United States to that of Russia, there was quite a variance in quality and progress. The higher quality and more progressive nature of American automobiles was achieved through competitive forces. Competitive forces can be applied to almost any environment, including Education and Religion. The individual is free to choose the optimal experience or decision as they see fit. Applied individually, competition allows the individual and their choices to be affirmed through merit-based achievements, fostering an environment in which rewards are based on skills and efforts alone. Inspired by their own set of desired experiences and achievements, individuals enter into a competition to realize the optimal quality of life as they themselves have defined it.

Competition contributes to the rapid advancement of society, just as it strengthens the **social fabric** of society. Competition allows for the individual's pursuit of their own goals and happiness at their own chosen level of investment, leaving them their earned reward. Competition is the mother of all—personal, societal, and global—progress. Competition, and the fostering of competition, are not just desirable; it is necessary.

Consistency

A crucial ingredient of **critical thinking** is **consistency**. In thinking critically about any issue, consistency acts as a litmus test to help determine whether analysis has been well applied. Think about it: Citizens cannot perceive inconsistent application of society's laws and rules. Roulette in upholding laws will result in roulette in breaking laws. The icon of the US judicial system is the symbol of the blindfolded jurist (**Lady Justice**) holding up the scales of **justice**, weighing the arguments and claims of both sides. The implication is that true justice is blind, as it is applied equally to all.

For the **fabric of society** to continually strengthen, consistency is required. While this example of consistency relates to laws, we find that consistency is a basic requirement in any number of environments in order to create and maintain **credibility**.

Leadership—Credibility and Inspiration

Here is an interesting quote from Peter F. Drucker (considered by some to be the dean of management theory): "Management is doing things right; leadership is doing the right things."

First, it needs to be acknowledged that pivotal events generate leaders. And sometimes these leaders—who were previously never thought of as being a **leader**—emerge when they are thrust into a situation. They take the mantle of responsibility and, with courage and conviction of virtue, rise to the occasion as true leaders.

Human beings often put a high priority on being part of a **winning team**. In surveys of personal achievement priorities, this desire to win and be among winners often ranks higher than simply earning an income. But who is the person starting this winning team? Starting this successful business? Starting this foundation? Someone must create the original ideas, making possible the opportunities for employment or involvement.

We usually deem the person at the top of an organization **the leader**—the first person to create the entity, the **founder**. And people may come to work for an organization—in most cases, they believe the organization to be **credible**, or credible enough that they are willing to associate themselves professionally. People may work for that entity, but they may not be **inspired**. So what is it that creates **inspiration**?

To be part of an organization and become dedicated to it typically requires a critical ingredient somewhere at or near the top of that organization. Just as there is a **fabric of society**, there is a **corporate culture** that has been created over time, either accidentally or with purpose. If the corporate culture at a company is outstanding—such that it fulfills the greater desire to be a member of the organization more than the desire to be a paid employee—then there is most likely excellent leadership at the top of the company, within a division, or within a department where a leader **inspires** subordinates.

From there it follows that to have the clearest picture of the desired corporate culture, we probably want to have the clearest understanding of the ingredients that make up the best leaders. We maintain, therefore, that the best characterization of the term **leadership** demands an understanding of the two terms that help define excellence within leadership: **credibility** and **inspiration**.

Credibility is closely tied to true inspiration. But you can have credibility without inspiration; contributing factors to inspiration go beyond credibility.

Credibility

Credibility can be created by some or all of the following (violation of any of these can ruin credibility):

1. **Integrity**. One does the right thing in all cases and does not take credit for others' efforts but rather recognizes them.

2. **Dependability.** If someone says they will do something, you can count on it being done.

3. **Consistency.** Treatment of people and policies is free from variation or contradiction.

4. **Teamwork.** Individuals put the team's goals and efforts ahead of personal desires.

5. **Determination and perseverance.** Not giving up until the task is completed.

6. **Selfless behavior (good teamwork)**

    * **With regard to society.** The leader puts the interests of society ahead of their own.

    * **With regard to the organization.** The leader puts the interests of the organization ahead of their own.

    * **With regard to individuals.** The leader assists others in realizing their full potential, which may put others' interests ahead of the leader's interests or responsibilities within the organization.

Inspiration

Inspiration can be created by some or all of the following (violation of any of these can ruin inspiration):

1. **Integrity.** The leader does the right thing in all cases and does not take credit for others' efforts but rather recognizes them.

- *"Commit to doing the right thing no matter the cost."*

- *"Speak truth to power."*

- *"Tell your people to take a stand on integrity and then stand up for them"* (Jim Cuminale, a former chief counsel at Nielsen)

2. **Dependability**
3. **Consistency**
4. **Teamwork**
5. **Determination and perseverance**
6. **Excellent communication and instruction skills**
7. **Charisma/chemistry.** The leader possesses a natural magnetism but is not attention-seeking.
8. **Selfless behavior (great teamwork)**

    - **With regard to society.** The leader puts the interests of society ahead of their own.

    - **With regard to the organization.** The leader puts the interests of the organization ahead of their own.

    - **With regard to individuals.** The leader assists others in realizing their full potential, which may put others' interests ahead of the leader's interests and responsibilities within the organization.

You may have noticed that **credibility** and **inspiration** are closely aligned. All these characteristics contribute to an individual's credibility and also their ability to be inspirational.

Validating episodes handed down in the lore of the organization contributes to and significantly strengthens the corporate/organizational culture. A true leader is looked up to by almost all. When this level of reverence is accomplished, the individual, as a true **leader** of individuals, is not merely the **manager** of subordinates.

It often seems as though those who work in government bureaucracy are accountable to no one. They work, they strive, they advocate, they obfuscate, and all too often, they work to resist oversight/management/leadership—regardless of the party in power—the "deep state." Participating in these kinds of bureaucratic power trips does not reflect true leadership.

Having true leaders can take us to a beneficial future. A person who allocates resources and ensures tasks get completed does not embody leadership. A person who pursues power for the purpose of attaining power is not a leader.

Execution is also essential. Peter Drucker, a guru of management theory, said:

> *Effective leadership is not about making speeches or being liked; leadership is defined by results, not attributes.*
>
> *Rank does not confer privilege or give power. It imposes responsibility.*

Finally, consider that true leadership is best represented by an inverted pyramid because the leader must recognize that the true function of all managers all the way to the top is to "facilitate the function (productivity) of the subordinate." After all, the reason to employ each additional person is to create more productivity and profitability. Therefore, the primary responsibility is to keep all subordinates as productive as possible—not to expand an empire.

Vision

Vision and leadership are not the same or interchangeable. A person can be a leader, and a person can be a visionary. A leader may be visionary, or they may not be. A visionary individual may be a leader, or they may not be. However, an organization that has a **visionary leader** is truly fortunate. The leader may not be creating visionary breakthroughs. But with true **vision skills**, the leader will be able to recognize the opportunity of **visions** as explained or invented by others.

Using the analogy of a compass rose with 360 degrees, we can better explain **True North Vision**. In the compass rose, there are four directional vectors. We can refer to them as **North (360)—positive; East (90) and West (270)—neutral; and South (180).** Organizational decisions can be very beneficial (**True North, 360**), very detrimental (**South, 180**), or neutral (**East or West, 90 or 270**—taking a lot of work but not accomplishing much). (For further thoughts on Quantum Leap Logic and the ability to measure vision, see appendix 6a.)

Following leadership and vision, organizational succession is a very important topic.

Finally, in each of our unique pursuits, we must determine whether we are trying to please others or our own internal value system. It may be helpful in doing so to remember the following phrase:

> Success is externally defined, while happiness is internally defined.

May your value system help you create your own personal vision of the unique path you will each pursue, understanding success, but seeking happiness.

The Role of the Litmus Test: What Incentive and Motivation System Does the Proposed Solution Put in Place for the Identified Problem?

A very useful test for determining the quality of a solution to a well-identified problem is to ask the preceding bolded question. By doing so, you may quickly be able to tell whether your suggested solution, through the incentive(s) provided, will naturally motivate the individual(s) to behave in a socially desired fashion.

If it is determined that other behaviors may be suggested through this analysis, then it indicates that more iterations must be worked through until a more optimal and acceptable solution is found.

APPENDIX 1B: "AN OBITUARY FOR COMMON SENSE"

This appendix uses the metaphor of an obituary to describe behaviors that Critical Thinkers will recognize as totally lacking consistent logic. It is important because it demonstrates inconsistency. For anything to be successful and long-term sustainable, it must be consistent. We would maintain that the powers of evil seek to sew this inconsistency so as to add confusion. Eventually, people don't know right from wrong; the social fabric continues to break down; and thus, the society fails. The globalists use the people who don't possess common sense to break down those who do over time.

> Today, we mourn the passing of a beloved old friend, Common Sense, who has been with us for many years.
>
> No one knows for sure how old he was since his birth records were long ago lost in bureaucratic red tape. He will be remembered as having cultivated such valuable lessons as:
>
> Knowing when to come in out of the rain;
>
> Why the early bird gets the worm;
>
> Life isn't always fair;
>
> And maybe it was my fault.
>
> Common Sense lived by simple, sound financial policies (don't spend more than you can earn) and reliable strategies (adults, not children, are in charge). His health began to deteriorate

rapidly when well-intentioned but overbearing regulations were set in place. Reports of a 6-year-old boy charged with sexual harassment for kissing a classmate; teens suspended from school for using mouthwash after lunch; and a teacher fired for reprimanding an unruly student, only worsened his condition.

Common Sense lost ground when parents attacked teachers for doing the job that they themselves had failed to do in disciplining their unruly children. It declined even further when schools were required to get parental consent to administer sun lotion or an aspirin to a student, but could not inform parents when a student became pregnant and wanted to have an abortion.

Common Sense lost the will to live as the churches became businesses, and criminals received better treatment than their victims. Common Sense took a beating when you couldn't defend yourself from a burglar in your own home, and the burglar could sue you for assault.

Common Sense finally gave up the will to live after a woman failed to realize that a steaming cup of coffee was hot. She spilled a little on her lap and was promptly awarded a huge settlement.

Common Sense was preceded in death . . .

by his parents, Truth and Trust,

by his wife, Discretion,

by his daughter, Responsibility,

and by his son, Reason.

He is survived by his 5 stepbrothers:

I Know My Rights

I Want It Now

Someone Else Is To Blame

I'm A Victim

Pay Me For Doing Nothing

Not many attended his funeral because so few realized he was gone. If you still remember him, pass this on. If not, join the majority and do nothing. (Widely used, source unknown)

APPENDIX 1C: "THE UNSINKABLE SHIP *TITANIC AMERICA*"

As stated in chapter 1, common sense is the ability to make sound judgments. One would not expect a lot of confusion about that. However, the following article lists items displaying a great deal of apparent confusion. Therefore, it would appear that many are experiencing significant difficulty in applying common sense. Read what follows below, and see if you draw a similar conclusion.

"The Unsinkable Ship *Titanic America*"

"One of my readers sent this to me this morning. I do not know the original source, but it speaks for many of us."

I woke up, and as I had my morning coffee, I realized that everything is about to change. No matter how I vote, no matter what I say, something evil has invaded our nation, and our lives are never going to be the same.

I have been confused by the hostility of family and friends. I look at people I have known all my life—so hate-filled that they agree with opinions they would never express as their own. I think that I may well have entered *The Twilight Zone*.

You can't justify this insanity. We have become a nation that has lost its collective mind!

1. If a man pretends to be a woman, you are required to pretend with him.

2. Somehow, it's un-American for the census to count how many Americans are in America.

3. Russians influencing our elections are bad, but illegals voting in our elections are good.

4. It was cool for Joe Biden to "blackmail" the president of Ukraine, but it's an impeachable offense if Donald Trump inquires about it.

5. Twenty is too young to drink a beer, but eighteen is old enough to vote.

6. People who have never owned slaves should pay slavery reparations to people who have never been slaves.

7. People who have never been to college should pay the debts of college students who took out huge loans for their degrees.

8. Immigrants with tuberculosis and polio are welcome, but you'd better be able to prove your dog is vaccinated.

9. Irish doctors and German engineers who want to emigrate to the U.S. must go through a rigorous vetting process, but any illiterate gang member who jumps the southern fence is welcome.

10. $5 billion for border security is too expensive, but $1.5 trillion for "free" health care is not.

11. If you cheat to get into college, you go to prison, but if you cheat to get into the country, you go to college for free.

12. People who say there is no such thing as gender are demanding a female president.

13. We see other countries going socialist and collapsing, but it seems like a great plan for us.

14. Some people are held responsible for things that happened before they were born, while others are not held responsible for what they are doing right now.

15. Criminals are caught and released to hurt more people, but stopping them is bad because it's a violation of THEIR rights.

16. And pointing out all this hypocrisy somehow makes us "racists"?!

Nothing makes sense anymore—no values, no morals, no civility. People are dying of a Chinese virus, but it's racist to refer to it as Chinese even though it began in China. We are clearly living in an upside-down world where right is wrong and wrong is right, where moral is immoral and immoral is moral, where good is evil and evil is good, where killing murderers is wrong, but killing innocent babies is right.

Wake up, America. The great unsinkable ship *Titanic America* has hit an iceberg, is taking on water, and is sinking fast. The choice is yours to make. What will it be? **Time is short—make your choice wisely!** (From "The Geller Report" by Pamela Geller, September. 8, 2024, original source unknown.)

APPENDIX 1D: JAVIER MILEI'S SPEECH TO THE WORLD ECONOMIC FORUM (WEF) JANUARY 17, 2024

This speech by Argentina President Milei puts into words what should be important to people who love freedom and don't want global elites trying to take over control of the world in the pursuit of their egotistical goals and agenda. If there is ever only one world order, there will be no competition to let the best ideas bubble to the top. Freedom will be a thing of the past.

To understand Argentina currently and some background on its decline, it is instructive to follow the logic of its president, Javier Milei, who was elected on November 19, 2023. He was invited to speak at the World Economic Forum's (WEF) annual gathering of global elites in Davos, Switzerland, on January 17, 2024.

WEF is headed by Klaus Schwab, a "super globalist" who seems to believe in the superiority of a totalitarian global entity run by elites and has attempted to utilize global NGO organizations like WHO—the World Health Organization—to realize his vision.

Javier Milei's speech was a wake-up call to the citizens of all sovereign countries. It was an amazing speech and is provided here in its entirety to highlight its quality and importance to all current and future generations.

Javier Milei's Speech at the World Economic Forum (January 17, 2024)

Good afternoon. Thank you very much.

Today, I'm here to tell you that the Western world is in danger. And it is in danger because those who are supposed to defend the values of the West are co-opted by a vision of the world that inexorably leads to socialism and thereby to poverty.

Unfortunately, in recent decades, the main leaders of the Western world have abandoned the model of freedom for different versions of what we call collectivism. Some have been motivated by well-meaning individuals who are willing to help others, and others have been motivated by the wish to belong to a privileged caste.

We're here to tell you that collectivist experiments are never the solution to the problems that afflict the citizens of the world. Rather, they are the root cause. Do believe me: no one is in a better place than us, Argentines, to testify to these two points.

Thirty-five years after we adopted the model of freedom, back in 1860, we became a leading world power. And when we embraced collectivism over the course of the last 100 years, we saw how our citizens started to become systematically impoverished, and we dropped to spot number 140 globally.

But before having the discussion, it would first be important for us to take a look at the data that demonstrate why free enterprise capitalism is not just the only possible system to end world poverty, but also that it's the only morally desirable system to achieve this.

If we look at the history of economic progress, we can see how between the year zero and the year 1800, approximately, world per capita GDP practically remained constant throughout the whole reference period.

If you look at a graph of the evolution of economic growth throughout the history of humanity, you would see a hockey stick graph—an exponential function that remained constant for 90% of the time and which was exponentially triggered starting in the 19th century.

The only exception to this history of stagnation was in the late 15th century, with the discovery of the American continent. But apart from this exception, throughout the whole period between the year zero and the year 1800, global per capita GDP stagnated.

Now, it's not just that capitalism brought about an explosion in wealth from the moment it was adopted as an economic system. But also, if you look at the data, what you will see is that growth continues to accelerate throughout the whole period.

And throughout the whole period between the year zero and the year 1800, the per capita GDP growth rate remains stable at around 0.02% annually—almost no growth. Starting in the 19th century with the Industrial Revolution, the compound annual growth rate was 0.66%. At that rate, in order to double per capita GDP, you would need some 107 years.

Now, if you look at the period between the year 1900 and the year 1950, the growth rate accelerated to 1.66% a year. So you no longer need 107 years to double per capita GDP—but 66. And if you take the period between 1950 and the year 2000, you will see that the growth rate was 2.1%, which would mean that in only 33 years, we could double the world's per capita GDP.

This trend, far from stopping, remains well alive today. If we take the period between the years 2000 and 2023, the growth rate again accelerated to 3% a year, which means that we could double world's per capita GDP in just 23 years.

That said, when you look at per capita GDP since the year 1800 until today, what you will see is that after the Industrial Revolution, global per capita GDP multiplied by over 15 times, which meant a boom in growth that lifted 90% of the global population out of poverty.

We should remember that by the year 1800, about 95% of the world's population lived in extreme poverty. That figure dropped to 5% by the year 2020, prior to the pandemic. The conclusion is obvious.

Far from being the cause of our problems, free trade capitalism as an economic system is the only instrument we have to end hunger, poverty, and extreme poverty across our planet. The empirical evidence is unquestionable.

Therefore, since there is no doubt that free enterprise capitalism is superior in productive terms, the left-wing doxa has attacked capitalism, alleging matters of morality, saying—that's what the detractors claim—that it's unjust. They say that capitalism is evil because it's individualistic, and that collectivism is good because it's altruistic. Of course, with the money of others.

So, they therefore advocate for social justice. But this concept, which in the developed world became fashionable in recent times, has been a constant in political discourse in my country for over 80 years. The problem is that social justice is not just, and it doesn't contribute to general well-being.

Quite the contrary, it's an intrinsically unfair idea because it's violent. It's unjust because the state is financed through taxation, and taxes are collected coercively. Or can any one of us say that we voluntarily pay taxes? This means that the state is financed through coercion, and the higher the tax burden, the higher the coercion and the lower the freedom.

Those who promote social justice start with the idea that the whole economy is a pie that can be shared differently. But that pie is not a given. It's wealth that is generated in what Israel Kirzner, for instance, calls a market discovery process.

If the goods or services offered by a business are not wanted, the business will fail unless it adapts to what the market is demanding. They will do well and produce more if they make a good quality product at an attractive price. So, the market is a discovery process in which capitalists will find the right path as they move forward.

But if the state punishes capitalists when they're successful and gets in the way of the discovery process, it will destroy their incentives, and the consequence is that they will produce less.

The pie will be smaller, and this will harm society as a whole. Collectivism, by inhibiting these discovery processes and hindering the appropriation of discoveries, ends up binding the hands of entrepreneurs and prevents them from offering better goods and services at a better price.

So, how come academia, international organizations, economic theorists, and politicians demonize an economic system that has not only lifted 90% of the world's population out of extreme poverty but has continued to do so at an accelerating pace?

Thanks to free trade capitalism, the world is now living its best moment. Never in all of mankind's or humanity's history has there been a time of greater prosperity than today. This is true for all. The world today has more freedom, is richer, more peaceful, and more prosperous. This is particularly true for countries that have more economic freedom and respect the property rights of individuals.

Countries that have more freedom are 12 times richer than those that are repressed. The lowest percentile in free countries is better off than 90% of the population in repressed countries. Poverty is 25 times lower, and extreme poverty is 50 times lower. Citizens in free countries live 25% longer than citizens in repressed countries.

Now, what do we mean when we talk about libertarianism? Let me quote the words of the greatest authority on freedom in Argentina, Professor Alberto Benegas Lynch Jr., who says that libertarianism is the unrestricted respect for the life project of others, based on the principle of non-aggression, in defense of the right to life, liberty, and property.

Its fundamental institutions are private property, markets free from state intervention, free competition, the division of labor, and social cooperation, in which success is achieved only by serving others with goods of better quality or at a better price.

In other words, successful capitalist business people are social benefactors who, far from appropriating the wealth of others, contribute to the general well-being. Ultimately, a successful entrepreneur is a hero.

And this is the model that we are advocating for the Argentina of the future—a model based on the fundamental principle of libertarianism: the defense of life, of freedom, and of property.

Now, if free enterprise, capitalism, and economic freedom have proven to be extraordinary instruments for ending poverty in the world, and we are now at the best time in the history of humanity, it is worth asking why I say that the West is in danger.

And I say this precisely because, in countries that should defend the values of the free market, private property, and the other institutions of libertarianism, sectors of the political and economic establishment are undermining the foundations of libertarianism—opening up the doors to socialism and potentially condemning us to poverty, misery, and stagnation.

It should never be forgotten that socialism is always and everywhere an impoverishing phenomenon that has failed in every country where it's been tried. It has been a failure economically, socially, and culturally—and it has also murdered over 100 million human beings.

The essential problem of the West today is not just that we need to come to grips with those who, even after the fall of the Berlin Wall and the overwhelming empirical evidence, continue to advocate for impoverishing socialism.

But there are also our own leaders, thinkers, and academics who rely on a misguided theoretical framework to undermine the fundamentals of the system that has given us the greatest expansion of wealth and prosperity in our history.

The theoretical framework to which I refer is that of Neoclassical economic theory, which designs a set of instruments that, unwillingly or without meaning to, end up serving state intervention, socialism, and social degradation.

The problem with Neoclassicals is that the model they fell in love with does not map reality, so they blame their mistakes on supposed market failures rather than reviewing the premises of their model.

Under the pretext of market failures, regulations are introduced. These regulations create distortions in the price system, prevent economic calculus, and therefore also prevent saving, investment, and growth.

This problem lies mainly in the fact that not even supposed libertarian economists understand what the market truly is. Because if they did understand, it would quickly become evident that it's impossible for market failures to exist.

The market is not merely a graph describing a curve of supply and demand. The market is a mechanism for social cooperation, where individuals voluntarily exchange ownership rights. Therefore, based on this definition, talking about a market failure is an oxymoron.

There are no market failures.

If transactions are voluntary, the only context in which there can be a market failure is if there is coercion—and the only entity that is able to coerce is the state, which holds a monopoly on violence.

Consequently, if someone considers that a market failure exists, I would suggest they check whether state intervention is involved. And if they find that it is not the case, I would suggest they check again—because obviously, there's a mistake.

Market failures do not exist.

An example of the so-called market failures described by the Neoclassicals is the concentrated structure of the economy. From the year 1800 onward, with the population multiplying by eight or nine times, per capita GDP grew by over 15 times, meaning there were growing returns that reduced extreme poverty from 95% to 5%.

However, the presence of growing returns involves concentrated structures, what we would call a monopoly. How, then, could something that has generated so much well-being be considered a market failure under Neoclassical theory?

Neoclassical economists need to think outside the box. When the model fails, you shouldn't get angry with reality—you should get angry with the model and change it.

The dilemma faced by the Neoclassical model is that they claim to wish to perfect the function of the market by attacking what they consider to be failures. But in doing so, they don't just open the doors to socialism—they also stifle economic growth.

For example, regulating monopolies, destroying their profits, and eliminating growing returns would automatically destroy economic growth.

However, faced with the theoretical demonstration that state intervention is harmful—and the empirical evidence that it has failed (which could not have been otherwise)—the solution proposed by collectivists is not greater freedom but rather greater regulation, creating a downward spiral of regulations until we are all poorer and our lives depend on a bureaucrat sitting in a luxury office.

Given the dismal failure of collectivist models and the undeniable advances of the free world, socialists were forced to change their agenda. They abandoned the class struggle based on the economic system and replaced it with other supposed social conflicts, which are just as harmful to life and economic growth.

The first of these new battles was the ridiculous and unnatural fight between men and women. Libertarianism already provides for equality of the sexes. The cornerstone of our creed is that all humans are created equal and that we all have the same inalienable rights granted by the Creator, including life, freedom, and ownership.

All that the radical feminist agenda has done is increase state intervention, hinder economic progress, and create jobs for bureaucrats who have not contributed anything to society—examples being ministries of women or international organizations devoted to promoting this agenda.

Another conflict presented by socialists is that of humans against nature, claiming that we human beings damage the planet and that it should be protected at all costs, even going so far as advocating for population control mechanisms or the abortion agenda.

Unfortunately, these harmful ideas have taken a stronghold in our society. Neo-Marxists have managed to co-opt the common sense of the Western world—and they have done this by seizing control of the media, culture, universities, and international organizations.

The last case is probably the most serious one because these institutions have enormous influence over the political and economic decisions of their member states.

Fortunately, there are more and more of us who dare to make our voices heard—because we see that if we don't truly and decisively fight against these ideas, the only possible outcome is that we will face increasing state regulation, socialism, poverty, and less freedom—and therefore, worse standards of living.

The West has, unfortunately, already started down this dangerous path.

I know—to many, it may sound ridiculous to suggest that the West has turned to socialism.

But this is only ridiculous if you limit yourself to the traditional economic definition of socialism, which states that it is an economic system where the state owns the means of production.

This definition, in my view, should be updated in light of current circumstances.

Today, states don't need to directly control the means of production to control every aspect of the lives of individuals.

With tools such as printing money, debt, subsidies, controlling interest rates, price controls, and regulations to correct so-called market failures, governments can exert control over the lives and fates of millions of individuals.

This is how we have arrived at the point where, under different names and disguises, a significant number of the generally accepted ideologies in most Western countries are collectivist variants—whether they proclaim to be openly communist, fascist, socialist, social democrats, national socialists, Christian democrats, neo-Keynesians, progressives, populists, nationalists, or globalists.

Ultimately, there are no major differences between them.

They all demand that the state steer every aspect of the lives of individuals.

They all defend a model that contradicts the one that led humanity to the most spectacular progress in its history.

We have come here today to invite the Western world to return to the path of prosperity.

Economic freedom, limited government, and unlimited respect for private property are essential elements for economic growth.

The impoverishment produced by collectivism is not a fantasy, nor is it an inescapable fate.

It is a reality that we Argentines know very well.

We have lived through this.

We have endured this because—as I said earlier—ever since we decided to abandon the model of freedom that made us rich, we have been caught up in a downward spiral—a spiral in which we are poorer and poorer, day by day.

This is something we have lived through—and we are here to warn you about what can happen if Western countries, which became rich through the model of freedom, continue on this path of servitude.

The case of Argentina is an empirical demonstration that no matter how rich you may be, no matter how many natural resources you have, no matter how skilled or educated your population is, no matter how much gold sits in your central bank—if a country adopts measures that hinder the free functioning of markets, competition, price systems, trade, and private property ownership, the only possible outcome is poverty.

Therefore, in conclusion, I would like to leave a message for all business people here and those who are not here in person but are following from around the world.

Do not be intimidated by the political caste or by parasites who live off the state. Do not surrender to a political class that only wants to stay in power and retain its privileges.

You are social benefactors.

You are heroes.

You are the creators of the most extraordinary period of prosperity we've ever seen.

Let no one tell you that your ambition is immoral. If you make money, it's because you offer a better product at a better price, thereby contributing to general well-being.

Do not surrender to the advance of the state.

The state is not the solution.

The state is the problem itself.

You are the true protagonists of this story.

And rest assured that, as of today, Argentina is your staunch and unconditional ally.

Thank you very much, and long live freedom!

APPENDIX 1E: COLORADO PAST GOVERNOR RICHARD LAMM ON THE EASE OF DESTROYING AMERICA

Governor Lamm, a Democrat, outlines the activities that could destroy the beacon of light that the United States represents. Contrast his following thoughts with what has occurred in recent years.

In the spring of 2005 (at an overpopulation conference in Washington, DC), Governor Richard Lamm of Colorado made the following points on how great nations commit suicide.

> If you believe that America is too smug, too self-satisfied, too rich, then let's destroy America. It is not that hard to do. No nation in history has survived the ravages of time. Arnold Toynbee observed that all great civilizations rise and fall and that "An autopsy of history would show that all great nations commit suicide."
>
> Here is how they do it. . . . [T]o destroy America, turn America into a bilingual or multi-lingual and bicultural country. History shows that no nation can survive the tension, conflict, and antagonism of two or more competing languages and cultures. It is a blessing for an individual to be bilingual; however, it is a curse for a society to be bilingual. The historical scholar, Seymour Lipset, put it this way: 'The histories of bilingual and bi-cultural societies that do not assimilate are histories of turmoil, tension, and tragedy.' Canada, Belgium, Malaysia, and Lebanon all confront crises of national existence in which minorities press for autonomy, if not independence.

Pakistan and Cyprus have divided. Europe confronts self-isolated Muslim communities.

Invent *multiculturalism* and encourage immigrants to maintain their culture. Make it an article of belief that all cultures are equal. That there are no cultural differences. Make it an article of faith that the Black and Hispanic dropout rates are due solely to prejudice and discrimination by the majority. Every other explanation is out of bounds.

> I would encourage all immigrants to keep their own language and culture. I would replace the melting pot metaphor with the salad bowl metaphor. It is important to ensure that we have various cultural subgroups living in America, enforcing their differences rather than as Americans, emphasizing their similarities.

> I would make our . . . growing demographic group(s) the least educated.

> [I would] get big foundations and businesses to give these efforts lots of money. I would invest in ethnic identity, and I would establish the cult of V*ictimology*. I would get all minorities to think that their lack of success was the fault of the majority. I would start a grievance industry blaming all minority failure on the majority population.

> I would place all subjects off limits; make it taboo to talk about anything against the cult of *diversity*. I would find a word similar to *heretic* in the 16th century that stopped discussion and paralyzed thinking. Words like *racist* or *xenophobe* halt

discussion and debate. Having made America a bilingual/bicultural country, having established multiculturalism, having large foundations fund the doctrine of Victimology, I would next make it impossible to enforce our immigration laws. I would develop a mantra: That because immigration has been good for America, it must always be good. I would make every individual immigrant symmetric and ignore the cumulative impact of millions of them. (Mike Zeller posting on LinkedIn, August 21, 2016)

APPENDIX 1F: THOUGHT-PROVOKING QUOTATIONS FROM THOMAS SOWELL AND MANY OTHERS

Over the millennia and recent centuries, individuals have been able to put very incisive thoughts into short phrases. Their quotes are very instructive in understanding the humans' participation in their society. Thomas Sowell begins this collection because of his prolific brilliance. The rest are in chronological order by that person's year of birth.

Thomas Sowell (1930–present)

Thomas Sowell is one of the most brilliant economists to grace our country with his presence. His quotes are pithy, brief, and full of meaning. In this book demonstrating the need for **critical thinking**, he exudes the premier example of just that through the following quotes. To understand Thomas Sowell and his road to personal development, we recommend the book *Maverick* by Jason Riley. The obstacles he overcame to become one of the premier economists of our time are almost a miracle and a case study of determination. Enjoy his following observations filled with wisdom.

> Without a moral framework, there is nothing left but immediate self-indulgence by some and the path of least resistance by others. Neither can sustain a free society.

> Freedom has cost too much blood and agony to be relinquished at the cheap price of rhetoric.

> Socialism has a record of failure so blatant that only an 'intellectual' could ignore or evade it.

Ours may become the first civilization destroyed, not by the power of our enemies, but by the ignorance of our teachers and the dangerous nonsense they are teaching our children.

Civil rights used to be about treating everyone the same. But today, some people are so used to special treatment that equal treatment is considered to be discrimination.

One of the sad signs of our times is that we have demonized those who produce, subsidized those who refuse to produce, and canonized those who complain.

The next time some academics tell you how important diversity is, ask how many conservatives there are in their sociology department.

Some of the biggest cases of mistaken identity are among intellectuals who have trouble remembering that they are not God.

What exactly is your fair share of what someone else has worked for?

I have never understood why it is "greed" to want to keep the money you have earned but not greed to want to take somebody else's money.

The real goal should be to reduce government spending, rather than increasing tax rates to cover ever-rising spending.

Much of the social history of the Western world over the past three decades has been a history of replacing what worked with what sounded good.

We seem to be getting closer and closer to a situation where nobody is responsible for what they did, but we are all responsible for what somebody else did.

Too much of what is called "education" is little more than an expensive isolation from reality.

The welfare state is the oldest con game in the world. First, you take people's money away quietly, and then you give some of it back to them flamboyantly.

The welfare state is not really about the welfare of the masses. It is about the egos of the elites.

It is hard to imagine a more stupid or more dangerous way of making decisions than by putting those decisions in the hands of people who pay no price for being wrong.

No society ever thrived because it had a large and growing class of parasites living off those who produce.

Sometimes it seems as if there are more solutions than problems. On closer scrutiny, it turns out that many of today's problems are a result of yesterday's solutions.

You'll never understand bureaucracies until you understand that for bureaucrats, procedure is everything and outcomes are nothing.

Open-ended demands are a mandate for ever-expanding bureaucracies with ever-expanding budgets and powers.

Most people who read *The Communist Manifesto* probably have no idea that it was written by a couple of young men who had never worked a day in their lives, and who nevertheless spoke boldly in the name of "the workers."

Envy was once considered to be one of the seven deadly sins before it became one of the most admired virtues under its new name, "social justice."

People will forgive you for being wrong, but they will never forgive you for being right—especially if events prove you right while proving them wrong.

The endlessly repeated argument that most Americans are the descendants of immigrants ignores the fact that most Americans are not the descendants of illegal immigrants.

Some Americans will never appreciate America until after they have helped destroy it and have begun to suffer the consequences.

The real motives of liberals have nothing to do with the welfare of other people. Instead, they have two related goals—to establish themselves as morally and intellectually superior to the rather distasteful population of common people, and to gather as much power as possible to tell those distasteful common people how they must live their lives.

OTHER THINKERS AND LEADERS

Lao Tzu (6th-entury BC)

A leader is best when people barely know he exists. When his work is done, his aim fulfilled, they will say: *We did it ourselves.*

Plato (427–347 BC)

If you do not take an interest in the affairs of your government, then you are doomed to live under the rule of fools.

Aristotle (384–322 BC)

Government should govern for the good of the people, not for the good of those in power.

Be a free thinker and don't accept everything you hear as truth. Be critical and evaluate what you believe in.

It is also a habit of tyrants to prefer the company of aliens to that of citizens at table and in society; citizens, they feel, are enemies, but aliens will offer no opposition.

The worst form of inequality is to try to make unequal things equal.

Alexander the Great (356–323 BC)

Remember, upon the conduct of each depends the fate of all.

Cicero (106–43 BC)

The first duty of man is the seeking after and the investigation of truth.

Seneca (4 BC–AD 65)

Luck is what happens when preparation meets opportunity.

Sir Isaac Newton (1642–1727)

What we know is a drop, what we don't know is an ocean.

Voltaire (1694– 1778)

No problem can withstand the assault of sustained thinking.

Benjamin Franklin (1706–1790)

This book's title is an allusion to the following quotation. On September 17, 1787, Elizabeth Willing Powel posed the question: "Well, Doctor, what have we got, a republic or a monarchy?"

To which Benjamin Franklin famously replied, "A republic, if you can keep it."

It is the first responsibility of every citizen to question authority.

Only a virtuous people are capable of freedom. As nations become corrupt and vicious, they have more need of masters.

Whoever would overthrow the liberty of a nation must begin by subduing the freeness of speech.

Security without liberty is called prison.

Common sense without education is better than education without common sense.

War is when the government tells you who the bad guy is. Revolution is when you decide that for yourself.

Motivation is when your dreams put on work clothes.

The best thing to give to your enemy is forgiveness; to an opponent, tolerance; to a friend, your heart; to your child, a good example; to a father, deference; to your mother, conduct that will make her proud of you; to yourself, respect; to all others, charity.

When you are good to others, you are best to yourself.

There are many roads to success, but only one sure road to failure, and that is to try to please everyone else.

Freedom is not a gift bestowed upon us by other men, but a right that belongs to us by the laws of God and nature.

Wise men don't need advice. Fools won't take it.

Samuel Adams (1722–1803)

Samuel Adams said in a speech to the **Second Continental Congress** on **August 1, 1776**:

> If ye love wealth greater than liberty, the tranquility of servitude greater than the animating contest for freedom, go home from us in peace. We ask not your counsel or arms. Crouch down and lick the hands which feed you. May your chains sit lightly upon you, and may posterity forget that ye were our countrymen.

George Washington (1732–1799)

Human happiness and moral duty are inseparably connected.

It is impossible to govern the world without God. It is the duty of all nations to acknowledge the providence of Almighty God, to obey His will, to be grateful for His benefits, and humbly to implore His protection and favor.

The future of this nation depends on the Christian training of our youth.

Religion and morality are essential pillars of civil society.

Truth will ultimately prevail where pains are taken to bring it to light.

Do not let anyone claim tribute of American patriotism if they even attempt to remove religion from politics.

You have only one way to convince others—listen to them.

Firearms stand next in importance to the Constitution itself."

To be prepared for war is one of the most effective means of preserving peace.

But if the laws are to be so trampled upon with impunity, and a minority is to dictate to the majority, there is an end put at one stroke to republican government, and nothing but anarchy and confusion is to be expected thereafter.

Occupants of public offices love power and are prone to abuse it.

Be Americans. Let there be no sectionalism—no North, South, East, or West. You are all dependent on one another and should be one in union. In one word, be a nation. Be Americans, and be true to yourselves.

The last official act of any government is to loot the treasury.

Patrick Henry (1736–1799)

You ought to be extremely cautious, watchful, jealous of your liberty; for instead of securing your rights, you may lose them forever.

Thomas Paine (1737–1809)

Those who want to reap the benefits of this great nation (The United States) must bear the fatigue of supporting it.

Moderation in temper is always a virtue, but moderation in principle is always a vice.

> Reason obeys itself, and ignorance submits to whatever is dictated to it.
>
> Some people can be reasoned into sense, and others must be shocked into it.
>
> To argue with a person who has renounced the use of reason is like administering medicine to the dead.

Thomas Jefferson (1743–1826)

President **John F. Kennedy**, **April 29, 1962**, in "Remarks at a Dinner Honoring Nobel Prize Winners of the Western Hemisphere":

> I think this is the most extraordinary collection of talent, of human knowledge, that has ever been gathered together at the White House, with the possible exception of when Thomas Jefferson dined alone. Someone once said that Thomas Jefferson was a gentleman of 32 who could calculate an eclipse, survey an estate, tie an artery, plan an edifice, try a cause, break a horse, and dance the minuet.

Jefferson Quotes

> If people let government decide which food they eat and medicines they take, their bodies will soon be in as sorry a state as are the souls of those who live under tyranny.

When the people are afraid of the government, there is tyranny. But when the government is afraid of the people, there is liberty.

When tyranny becomes law, rebellion becomes duty.

The natural progress of things is for liberty to yield and government to gain ground. One of the most profound preferences in human nature is for satisfying one's needs and desires with the least possible exertion; for appropriating wealth produced by the labor of others, rather than producing it by one's own labor. The stronger and more centralized the government, the safer would be the guarantee of such monopolies; in other words, the stronger the government, the weaker the producer, the less consideration need be given him, and the more might be taken away from him.

The issue today is the same as it has been throughout all history—whether man shall be allowed to govern himself or be ruled by a small elite.

There is no justification for taking away an individual's freedom in the guise of public safety.

A true patriot will defend his country from its government.

When you abandon freedom to achieve security, you lose both and deserve neither.

When once a republic is corrupted, there is no possibility of remedying any of the growing evils but by removing the corruption and restoring its lost principles; every other correction is either useless or a new evil.

The end of democracy and the defeat of the American Revolution will occur when government falls into the hands of the lending institutions and moneyed incorporations.

Laws that forbid the carrying of arms . . . disarm only those who are neither inclined nor determined to commit crimes . . . Such laws make things worse for the assaulted and better for the assailants. They serve rather to encourage than to prevent homicides, for an unarmed man may be attacked with greater confidence than an armed man.

Free men do not ask permission to bear arms.

Whenever any form of government becomes destructive of these ends (life, liberty, and the pursuit of happiness), it is the right of the people to alter or abolish it and institute new government.

A private central bank issuing the public currency is a greater menace to the liberties of the people than a standing army. We must not let our rulers load us with perpetual debt.

The federal government is our servant, not our master.

The government you elect is the government you deserve.

To learn, you have to listen. To improve, you have to try.

Evil triumphs when good men do nothing.

Men of quality are not threatened by women of equality.

The press is impotent when it abandons itself to falsehood.

I never considered a difference of opinion in politics, in religion, or in philosophy as a cause for withdrawing from a friend.

Peace is the brief, glorious moment in history when everybody stands around reloading.

Equal rights for all, special privileges for none.

The tree of liberty must be refreshed from time to time with the blood of patriots and tyrants.

Who will govern the governors? There is only one force in the nation that can be depended upon to keep the government pure and the governors honest, and that is the people themselves. They alone, if well informed, are capable of preventing the corruption of power and of restoring the nation to its rightful course if it should go astray. They alone are the safest depository of the ultimate power of government.

A well-informed citizenry is the best defense against tyranny.

James Madison (1751–1836)

It will be of little avail to the people if the laws be so voluminous that they cannot be read, or so incoherent that they cannot be understood.

Alexander Hamilton (1755–1804)

Give all the power to the many, they will oppress the few. Give all power to the few, they will oppress the many.

Harriet Martineau (1802–1876)

Readers are plentiful; thinkers are rare.

Abraham Lincoln (1809–1865)

Those who deny freedom to others deserve it not for themselves.

We the people are the rightful masters of both Congress and the courts, not to overthrow the Constitution but to overthrow the men who pervert the Constitution.

America will never be destroyed from the outside. If we falter and lose our freedoms, it will be because we destroyed ourselves.

Great men are ordinary men with extraordinary determination.

Nearly all men can stand adversity, but if you want to test a man's character, give him power.

You must remember that some things legally right are not morally right.

Better to remain silent and be thought a fool than to speak out and remove all doubt.

Sir, my concern is not whether God is on our side; my greatest concern is to be on God's side, for God is always right.

We have been preserved, these many years, in peace and prosperity. We have grown in numbers, wealth, and power, as no other nation has ever grown. But we have forgotten God. We have forgotten the gracious hand that preserved us in peace, and multiplied and enriched and strengthened us; and we have vainly imagined, in the deceitfulness of our hearts, that all these blessings were produced by some superior wisdom and virtue of our own. Intoxicated with unbroken success, we have become too self-sufficient to feel the necessity of redeeming and preserving Grace, too proud to pray to the God that made us!

It is a sin to be silent when it is your duty to protest.

You cannot build character and courage by taking away people's initiative and independence. You cannot help people permanently by doing for them what they could and should do for themselves.

You cannot help the poor by destroying the rich. You cannot lift the wage earner by pulling down the wage payer.

Discipline is choosing between what you want now, and what you want most.

A day spent helping no one but yourself is a day wasted.

I am a firm believer in the people. If given the truth, they can be depended upon to meet any national crisis. The great point is to bring them the real facts.

We can complain because rose bushes have thorns, or rejoice because thorn bushes have roses.

In the end, it's not the years in your life that count. It's the life in your years.

Vladimir Lenin (1870–1924)

The goal of socialism is communism.

Winston Churchill (1874–1965)

Socialism is a philosophy of failure, the creed of ignorance, and the gospel of envy; its inherent virtue is the equal sharing of misery.

The inherent vice of capitalism is the unequal sharing of blessings; the inherent virtue of socialism is the equal sharing of miseries.

Many forms of Government have been tried, and will be tried, in this world of sin and woe. No one pretends that democracy is perfect or all-wise. Indeed it has been said that democracy is the worst form of Government except for all those other forms that have been tried from time to time . . .

Albert Einstein (1879–1955)

Education is not the learning of facts, but the training of the mind to think.

Learn from yesterday, live for today, hope for tomorrow. The important thing is not to stop questioning.

Two things are infinite: the universe and human stupidity; and I'm not sure about the universe.

C. S. Lewis (1898–1963)

If you look for truth, you may find comfort in the end; if you look for comfort, you will not get either comfort or truth— only soft soap and wishful thinking to begin, and in the end, despair.

The greatest evils in the world will not be carried out by men with guns, but by men in suits sitting behind desks.

Of all tyrannies, a tyranny sincerely exercised for the good of its victims may be the most oppressive.

Ayn Rand (1905–1982)

Devotion to the truth is the hallmark of morality; there is no greater, nobler, more heroic form of devotion than the act of a man who assumes the responsibility of thinking.

Fascism and Communism are not two opposites, but two rival gangs fighting over the same territory—both are variants of statism, based on the collectivist principle that man is the rightless slave of the state.

There is no difference between Communism and Socialism, except in the means of achieving the same ultimate end: Communism proposes to enslave men by force, Socialism—by vote. It is merely the difference between murder and suicide.

When you see that, in order to produce, you need to obtain permission from men who produce nothing—when you see that money is flowing to those who deal not in goods but in favors—when you see that men get richer by graft and by pull than by work, and your laws don't protect you against them but protect them against you—when you see corruption being rewarded and honesty becoming a self-sacrifice—you may know that your society is doomed.

What is greatness? I will answer: it is the capacity to live by the three fundamental values of John Galt: reason, purpose, and self-esteem.

Peter Drucker (1909–2005)

Effective leadership is not about making speeches or being liked; leadership is defined by results, not attributes.

Rank does not confer privilege or give power. It imposes responsibility.

Management is doing things right; leadership is doing the right things.

Ronald Reagan (1911–2004)

Freedom is never more than one generation away from extinction. We didn't pass it on to our children in the bloodstream. The only way they can inherit the freedom we have known is if we fight for it, protect it, defend it, and then hand it to them with the well-fought lessons of how they, in their lifetime, must do the same. And if you and I don't do this, then you and I may well spend our sunset years telling our children and our children's children what it once was like in America when men were free. (1961)

One of the traditional methods of imposing statism or socialism on a people has been by way of medicine. It's very easy to disguise a medical program as a humanitarian project. (1961)

If we lose freedom here, there is no place to escape to. This is the last stand on Earth. And this idea—that government is beholden to the people, that it has no other source of power except the sovereign people—is still the newest and most unique idea in all the long history of man's relation to man. This is the issue of this election: whether we believe in our capacity for self-government or whether we abandon the American Revolution and confess that a little intellectual elite in a far-distant capital can plan our lives for us better than we can plan them ourselves. (1964)

Government is like a baby: an alimentary canal with a big appetite at one end and no responsibility at the other. (1965)

There are those in America today who have come to depend absolutely on government for their security. And when government fails, they seek to rectify that failure in the form of granting government more power. So, as government has failed to control crime and violence with the means given it by the Constitution, they seek to give it more power at the expense of the Constitution. But in doing so, in their willingness to give up their arms in the name of safety, they are really giving up their protection from what has always been the chief source of despotism—government. (1975)

Lord Acton said power corrupts. Surely then, if this is true, the more power we give the government, the more corrupt it will become. And if we give it the power to confiscate our arms, we also give up the ultimate means to combat that corrupt power. In doing so, we can only assure that we will eventually be totally subject to it. When dictators come to power, the first thing they do is take away the people's weapons. It makes it so much easier for the secret police to operate—it makes it so much easier to force the will of the ruler upon the ruled. (1975)

The size of the federal budget is not an appropriate barometer of social conscience or charitable concern. (1981)

If the big spenders get their way, they'll charge everything on your Taxpayers Express Card. And believe me, they never leave home without it. (1984)

If we look to the answer as to why for so many years we achieved so much, prospered as no other people on Earth, it was because here in this land we unleashed the energy and individual genius of man to a greater extent than has ever been done before. Freedom and the dignity of the individual have been more available and assured here than in any other place on Earth. (1981)

Government's first duty is to protect the people, not run their lives. (1981)

In this present crisis, government is not the solution to our problem; government is the problem. From time to time we've been tempted to believe that society has become too complex to be managed by self-rule, that government by an elite group is superior to government for, by, and of the people. Well, if no one among us is capable of governing himself, then who among us has the capacity to govern someone else? (1981)

We are a nation that has a government—not the other way around. And this makes us special among the nations of the Earth. Our government has no power except that granted it by the people. It is time to check and reverse the growth of government, which shows signs of having grown beyond the consent of the governed. (1981)

It is time for us to realize that we're too great a nation to limit ourselves to small dreams. We're not, as some would have us believe, doomed to an inevitable decline. I do not believe in a fate that will fall on us no matter what we do. I do believe in a fate that will fall on us if we do nothing. So, with all the creative energy at our command, let us begin an era of national renewal. Let us renew our determination, our courage, and our strength. And let us renew our faith and our hope. We have every right to dream heroic dreams. Those who say that we're in a time when there are no heroes—they just don't know where to look. (1981)

Government's view of the economy could be summed up in a few short phrases: If it moves, tax it. If it keeps moving, regulate it. And if it stops moving, subsidize it. (1986)

How do you tell a Communist? Well, it's someone who reads Marx and Lenin. And how do you tell an anti-Communist? It's someone who understands Marx and Lenin. (1987)

The nine most terrifying words in the English language are: "I'm from the government, and I'm here to help." (1986)

You can't be for big government, big taxes, and big bureaucracy and still be for the little guy. (1988)

I hope we once again have reminded people that man is not free unless government is limited. There's a clear cause and effect here that is as neat and predictable as a law of physics: As government expands, liberty contracts. (1989)

Whatever else history may say about me when I'm gone, I hope it will record that I appealed to your best hopes, not your worst fears; to your confidence rather than your doubts. My dream is that you will travel the road ahead with liberty's lamp guiding your steps and opportunity's arm steadying your way. (1989)

Let's close the place down and see if anybody notices. (1995, on the federal government shutdown)

Nicolas Gomez Davila (1913–1994)

Violence is not necessary to destroy a civilization. Each civilization dies from indifference toward the unique values which created it.

Hierarchies are celestial. In hell, all are equal.

The church used to absolve sinners; today, it has the gall to absolve sins.

Nowadays, public opinion is not the sum of private opinions. On the contrary, private opinions are an echo of public opinion.

Truth is in history, but history is not the truth.

John Fitzgerald Kennedy (1917–1963)

Communism has never come to power in a country that was not disrupted by war or corruption or both.

Ask not what your country can do for you. Ask what you can do for your country.

Leadership and learning are indispensable to each other.

Aleksandr Solzhenitsyn (1918–2008)

Human beings are born with different capacities. If they are free, they are not equal. And if they are equal, they are not free.

William Arthur Ward (1921–1994)

The mediocre teacher tells. The good teacher explains. The superior teacher demonstrates. The great teacher inspires.

Margaret Thatcher (1925–2013)

Watch your thoughts for they will become actions. Watch your actions, for they'll become . . . habits. Watch your habits for they will forge your character. Watch your character, for it will make your destiny.

Martin Luther King Jr. (1929–1968)

I have a dream that my four little children will one day live in a nation where they will not be judged by the color of their skin but by the content of their character.

It is always the right time to do the right thing.

Injustice anywhere is a threat to justice everywhere.

Ben Carson (1951–present)

We've been conditioned to think that only politicians can solve our problems. But at some point, maybe we will wake up and recognize that it was the politicians who created our problems.

Elon Musk (1971–present)

> Propaganda isn't just about creating fake news. It's also about hiding real news.

Edward Snowden (1983–present)

> People don't realize how hard it is to speak the truth to a world full of people that don't realize they're living a lie.

J. Kevin Dolan (Coauthor of this book)

> Capitalism harnesses the power of the pursuit of self-interest.

> The economic system serves at the convenience of the political system.

> Critical thinking is the foundational thought process for the development of humankind.

> Have you identified a symptom or the true problem before creating a solution?

> What incentive and motivation system does the proposed solution put in place for the identified problem or issue?

> Success is externally defined, and Happiness is internally defined.

The Inverted Pyramid demonstrates the principle of a manager's responsibility to facilitate the function (productivity) of the subordinate.

APPENDIX 2A: EDUCATION—INTERNAL PUBLIC SCHOOL COMPETITION MECHANICS

This appendix offers the outline for a potentially innovative technique to create competition in the current public school system, where it does not currently exist today.

Eliminate wasted expenses such as busing.

Employ **two** principals, each with an assistant, at each school to head up **two** separate teams (e.g., Red and Green).

Placing Teachers into the Two Teams:

1. Flip a coin, and the winning principal gets the first choice of a teacher to have on their team.

2. After that, each principal gets two picks until the placement process is complete.

3. Any remaining teacher openings are filled by each principal respectively selecting teachers out in the open marketplace.

Placing Children in Classrooms:

At the end of each school year, attempt to place children where parents want them.

Step 1: Assign students to a specific teacher based on parental preference. If that teacher is unavailable (full class or no longer at the school), move to step 2.

Step 2: Place the child with a teacher from the parent's chosen team—Red or Green.

This process determines the number of team positions selected by the parents or guardians.

At the end of each succeeding year, based on the positions to be filled by each team:

- The losing team uses its system for attrition (if under a labor contract, according to contract rules).

- The gaining team goes to the marketplace and hires the best teacher(s) available. This **can** include teachers let go by the losing team, but does **not** require it. The losing team could lose some of its best teachers if a seniority system is used for attrition.

If any team is eventually reduced to a predetermined percentage of teaching positions (e.g., **20 percent or 25 percent**), then that team ceases to exist, and the process is repeated, starting with the following:

1. The selection of a new principal and assistant for the new team.

2. The selection of teachers for each team.

3. The **principal and assistant** of the dissolved team lose their jobs.

A **new principal** is selected by the **board of education** from the open marketplace—**not** by labor contracts or within the teacher union covering either existing team.

The **new principal hires an assistant** and leads their team in the teacher selection process.

Parents' wishes for the placement of their children are honored as much as feasible.

The **recall of a principal** may be set in motion by a **petition signed by a minimum of 25 percent of students' parents/guardians**.

Collusion between principals is illegal and, therefore, a **criminal activity**.

APPENDIX 5A: TUCKER CARLSON AND BRET WEINSTEIN DISCUSS THE WORLD HEALTH ORGANIZATION'S ATTEMPT TO REDUCE AMERICAN SOVEREIGNTY

This appendix informs readers of international efforts to reduce the absolute sovereignty of nations and the United States in particular. This attempt must be guarded against if citizens of countries want to remain free instead of being overseen by a global elite.

From *American Wire*, January 6, 2024, within Bo Snerdley's *Afternoon BS Alert*:

Weinstein said:

> The ability of WHO to "end the First Amendment in the United States" is currently under discussion at the international level.
>
> It's almost impossible to exaggerate how troubling what is being discussed is. In fact, I think it is fair to say that we are in the middle of a coup. We are actually facing the elimination of our national and our personal sovereignty.
>
> The modifications to WHO's pandemic preparedness plan have been intentionally crafted "in such a way that your eyes are supposed to glaze over as you attempt to sort out what is it. What is under discussion?"
>
> If we collectively zone out and ignore what WHO is attempting to do, then come May of this year, your nation is almost certain to sign on to an agreement that, in some utterly, vaguely described future circumstance, a public health emergency—which the director-general of the World Health

Organization has total liberty to define in any way that he sees fit—will trigger its provisions.

In other words, nothing prevents climate change from being declared a public health emergency that would trigger the provisions of these modifications. And in the case that some emergency or some pretense of an emergency shows up, the provisions that would kick in are beyond jaw-dropping.

Far from "minor and procedural" modifications, under the changes, WHO and its signatory nations will be allowed to define a public health emergency.

Having declared one, they will be entitled to mandate remedies. Remedies that are named include vaccines. Gene therapy technology is literally named in the set of things that the World Health Organization is going to reserve the right to mandate.

[WHO] will be in a position to require these things of citizens. It will be in a position to dictate our ability to travel—in other words, passports that would be predicated on one having accepted these technologies are clearly being described.

People's ability to choose their treatments would also disappear.

It would have the ability to forbid the use of other medications," Weinstein revealed. "So, this looks like they're preparing for a rerun where they can just simply take ivermectin, hydroxychloroquine off the table.

And then there are those pesky podcasters.

They also have reserved the ability to dictate how these measures are discussed. that censorship is described here as well—the right to dictate that.

Of course, "misinformation" is how they're going to describe it.

Tedros has no problem looking into a camera and lying to people, as proven by his recent remarks on the pandemic plan. Calling him out on it is an example of "malinformation," defined by the Department of Homeland Security (DHS) as "things that are based in truth that cause you to distrust authority."

According to DHS, it, along with misinformation and disinformation, is an act of "terrorism."

I should point out, as funny as that is, and as obviously Orwellian as that is, it's also terrifying because if you have tracked the history of the spreading tyranny from the beginning of the war on terror, you know that "terrorism" is not a normal English word the way it once was. Terrorism is now a legal designation that causes all of your rights to evaporate.

So, at the point that the Department of Homeland Security says that you are guilty of a kind of terrorism for saying true things that cause you to distrust your government, they are also telling you something about what rights they have to silence you. They are not normal rights. So, these things are all terrifying.

"My jaw's open," a wide-eyed Carlson stated.

But Weinstein wasn't done. He continued:

The COVID pandemic caused us to become aware of a lot of structures that had been built around us, something that former NSA officer William Binney once described as "the turnkey totalitarian state." The totalitarian state is erected around you. But it's not activated. And then once it's built, the key gets turned.

And so, we are now seeing, I believe, something that even outstrips William Binney's description because it's the turnkey totalitarian planet. I think the World Health Organization is above the level of nations, and it is going to be in a position, if these provisions pass, to dictate to nations how they are to treat their own citizens, to override their constitutions, despite what Tedros has told you.

As positively dismal as all this sounds, Weinstein still has hope for humanity's future.

Humanity is depending on everybody who has a position from which to see what is taking place, to grapple with what it might mean, and to describe it so that the public understands where their interests are. It is depending on us to do what needs to be done if we're to have a chance of delivering a planet to our children and our grandchildren that is worthy of them. If we're going to deliver a system that allows them to live meaningful, healthy lives, we have to speak up.

They are ferociously powerful. But, I would also point out this interesting error.

So, I call the force that we're up against "Goliath," just so I remember what the battle is. Goliath made a terrible mistake and made it most egregiously during COVID. It took all of the competent people, took all of the courageous people, and shoved them out of the institutions where they were hanging on.

And in so doing, it created *The Dream Team*. It created every player you could possibly want on your team to fight some historic battle against a terrible evil.

All of those people are now at least somewhat awake.. They've now been picked on by the same enemy. And yeah, all right, we're outgunned. It has a tremendous amount of power. But we've got all of the people who know how to think. I don't think it's a slam dunk, but I like our odds.

APPENDIX 5B: VOTING AND INDIVIDUAL RESPONSIBILITIES

This appendix considers the responsibilities and constraints around voting and carrying out the provisions of the Constitution.

It is the responsibility of the individual within their society—based on the governance of, by, and for the people—to exercise their privilege to vote for candidates who will operate the levers of governmental power to uphold the proper execution of the Constitution as it is written.

Should representatives or the executive branch refuse to execute the provisions of the Constitution as written, it is their obligation to pass legislation, up to and including Constitutional Amendments, to alter the provisions to a more acceptable and usable form. Until then, it is not a choice whether or not to execute the provisions. They must be executed.

Failure to do so is a violation of the Oath of Office and, as such, warrants removal from office through the existing mechanisms in place. Not upholding the Constitution through "blatant" (potentially defined) actions should be specifically recognized as an "impeachable offense."

Fraudulent voting in any form must carry severe penalties to deter individuals from fraudulently impacting election results and ballot initiatives.

Countries fight wars over their borders. Does it then make sense to ignore your own borders while giving aid to other country's protection of their borders? Furthermore, does it make sense to allow foreigners to freely cross and participate in your country's governance by voting? They have no "skin in the game." They have not earned the right to participate—that right comes with citizenship and requires passing citizenship tests (unless naturally born a citizen).

Would we, as United States citizens, expect to be allowed to vote when we fly into France or any other country? Other nations may welcome us as tourists to spend money on their services, but we would not possess sufficient knowledge of the national issues being contested. The citizens of that country do not want foreigners determining representative outcomes—voting with no negative consequences to themselves, yet with potentially big consequences for the citizens of that country.

Even legal immigrants who desire to become citizens should not vote until they have attained citizenship. However, these legal immigrants can still voice their opinions and exercise their right to free speech while not being allowed to vote and not leading demonstrations until they are a citizen.

When left-wing politicians in power pay billions of dollars to help Ukraine defend its borders while simultaneously opening our own borders and facilitating voter registration for illegal immigrants, the inconsistency is so glaring that it could be considered a criminal act.

When the same government offers $750 to American citizens whose lives have been devastated by Hurricane Helene while giving thousands of dollars and free shelter to illegal immigrants, common sense tells us that the citizens of this country are being blatantly abused.

Such actions should signal to every common citizen that the republic is at risk, and they must diligently exercise their right to vote to elect representatives who will put the country back on the right track.

APPENDIX 5C: JAVIER MILEI'S SPEECH TO THE UNITED NATIONS ON SEPTEMBER 24, 2024

Argentina's president once again wonderfully makes the case for populism versus the global elite's efforts.

> To the authorities of the United Nations, to the representatives of the various countries that make up the United Nations, and to all the citizens of the world who are watching us, good afternoon.
>
> For those who do not know, I am not a politician. I am an economist—a liberal libertarian economist—who has never had the ambition to be a politician and who was honored with the position of President of the Argentine Republic in the face of the resounding failure of more than a century of collectivist policies, a century of collectivist policies that destroyed our country.
>
> This is my first speech in front of the United Nations General Assembly, and I would like to take this opportunity to—with humility—alert the various nations of the world to the path they have been treading for decades and the danger of this organization's failure to fulfill its original mission.
>
> I do not come here to tell the world what to do; I come here to tell the world, on the one hand, what will happen if the United Nations continues to promote collectivist policies, which they have been promoting under the mandate of the

2030 Agenda, and, on the other hand, what are the values that the new Argentina defends.

I do want to begin by giving credit where credit is due. The United Nations organization was born out of the horror of the bloodiest war in global history, with the main objective that it should never happen again. To that end, the organization set its fundamental principles in stone in the Universal Declaration of Human Rights. A basic agreement was set down there, based on a maxim: that all human beings are born free and equal in dignity and rights.

Under the tutelage of this organization and the adoption of these ideas, during the last 70 years, humanity experienced the longest period of global peace in history, which also coincided with the period of the greatest economic growth in history. An international forum was created where nations could settle their conflicts through cooperation instead of resorting instantly to arms, and something unthinkable was achieved: the five largest powers in the world were permanently seated at the same table, each with the same veto power, despite having totally opposing interests.

All this did not make the scourge of war disappear, but it was achieved—for the time being—that no conflict escalated to global proportions. The result was that we went from having two world wars in less than 40 years, which together claimed more than 120 million lives, to having 70 consecutive years of relative peace and global stability, under the mantle of an order that allowed the whole world to integrate commercially, compete, and prosper. Because where there is trade, there are no bullets—Bastiat used to say—because trade guarantees peace, freedom guarantees trade, and equality before the law guarantees freedom.

In short, what the Prophet Isaiah wrote and what is read in the park, across the street, was fulfilled:

"God will judge between the nations and will arbitrate for many peoples; they will beat their swords into plowshares and their spears into pruning shears. Nation shall not take sword against nation; they shall know war no more."

This is what has happened—mostly—under the aegis of the United Nations in its first decades, and therefore, from this perspective, we are talking about a remarkable success in the history of nations that cannot be overlooked. However—at some point—and as it usually happens with most of the bureaucratic structures that we men create, this organization ceased to watch over the principles outlined in its founding declaration and began to mutate. An organization that had been intended—essentially—as a shield to protect the Kingdom of Man was transformed into a multi-tentacled Leviathan, which seeks to decide not only what each nation-state should do but also how all the citizens of the world should live. This is how we went from an organization that pursued peace to an organization that imposes an ideological agenda on its members, on a myriad of issues, which make up the life of man in society.

The successful model of the United Nations, whose origins can be traced back to the ideas of President Wilson, who spoke of the society of "peace without victory" and which was based on the cooperation of nation-states, has been abandoned; it has been replaced by a model of supranational government of international bureaucrats who seek to impose a certain way of life on the citizens of the world. What is being discussed—this week, here, in New York, at the Summit of the Future—is nothing other than the deepening of this tragic course that this institution has adopted. Thus, the deepening of a model that—in the words of the Secretary of the United Nations himself—requires the definition of a new social contract on a global scale, redoubling the commitments of the 2030 Agenda.

I want to be clear on the position of the Argentine agenda: the 2030 Agenda, although well-intentioned in its goals, is nothing more than a supranational government program, socialist in nature, which seeks to solve the problems of modernity with solutions that violate the sovereignty of nation-states and violate people's right to life, liberty, and property. It is an agenda that pretends to solve poverty, inequality, and discrimination with legislation that only deepens them. World history shows that the only way to guarantee prosperity is by limiting the power of the monarch, guaranteeing equality before the law, and defending the right to life, liberty, and property of individuals.

It has been precisely the adoption of this agenda, which obeys privileged interests, and the abandonment of the principles outlined in the Universal Declaration of Human Rights of the United Nations, that has distorted the role of this institution and put it on the wrong path. Thus, we have seen how an organization, born to defend the rights of man, has been one of the main proponents of the systematic violation of freedom—for example—with the global quarantines during the year 2020, which should be considered a crime against humanity.

In this same House that claims to defend human rights, they have allowed bloody dictatorships such as Cuba and Venezuela to join the Human Rights Council without the slightest reproach. In this same House that claims to defend women's rights, they allow countries that punish their women for showing their skin to join the Committee on the Elimination of Discrimination against Women. In this same House—systematically—they have voted against the State of Israel, which is the only country in the Middle East that defends liberal democracy, while simultaneously demonstrating a total inability to respond to the scourge of terrorism.

In the economic sphere, collectivist policies have been promoted that threaten economic growth, violate property rights, and hinder the natural economic process, preventing the most underprivileged countries in the world from freely enjoying their own resources in order to move forward. Regulations and prohibitions are promoted precisely by the countries that developed thanks to doing the same thing they condemn today. Moreover, a toxic relationship has been promoted between global governance policies and international lending agencies, requiring the most neglected countries to commit resources they do not have to programs they do not need, turning them into perpetual debtors to promote the agenda of the global elites.

Nor has the tutelage of the World Economic Forum helped, where ridiculous policies are promoted with Malthusian blinders on—such as "Zero Emission" policies—which harm poor countries in particular. Policies linked to sexual and reproductive rights are also promoted, even when the birth rate in Western countries is plummeting, heralding a bleak future for all.

 Nor has the organization satisfactorily fulfilled its mission of defending the territorial sovereignty of its members, as we Argentines know firsthand, in its relationship with the Malvinas Islands. We have even reached a situation in which the Security Council, which is the most important organ of this House, has become distorted because the veto of its permanent members has begun to be used in defense of the particular interests of some.

Thus, today we find ourselves with an organization that is powerless to provide solutions to real global conflicts, such as the aberrant Russian invasion of Ukraine, which has already cost the lives of more than 300,000 people, leaving a trail of more than one million wounded in the process. An organization that, instead of confronting these conflicts, invests time and effort in imposing on poor countries what, how, and what they should produce, with whom they should associate, what they should eat, and what they should believe in, as the present Pact for the Future intends to dictate.

This long list of errors and contradictions has not been without consequences. It has resulted in the loss of credibility of the United Nations in the eyes of the citizens of the free world and in the denaturalization of its functions.

Therefore, I would like to issue a warning: we are at the end of a cycle. Collectivism and moral posturing, along with the woke agenda, have collided with reality and no longer have credible solutions to offer to the world's real problems. In fact, they never had them. If the 2030 Agenda failed—as its own promoters acknowledge—the answer should be to ask ourselves if it was not an ill-conceived program, to begin with, accept that reality, and change course. We cannot persist in the mistake of doubling down on an agenda that has failed. The same thing always happens with ideas coming from the left: they design a model according to what human beings **should be**, in their view, and when individuals **freely** act otherwise, they have no better solution than to restrict, repress, and limit their freedom.

We—in Argentina—have already seen with our own eyes what lies at the end of this road of envy and sad passions: poverty, brutalization, anarchy, and a fatal absence of freedom. We still have time to turn away from this course.

I want to be clear about something so that there are no misinterpretations: Argentina, which is undergoing a profound process of change, has decided to embrace the ideas of freedom—those ideas that say that all citizens are born free and equal before the law, that we have inalienable rights granted by the Creator, among which are the right to life, liberty, and property. Those principles, which guide the process of change that we are carrying out in Argentina, are also the principles that will guide our international conduct from now on.

We believe in the defense of life for all.

We believe in the defense of property for all.

We believe in freedom of speech for all.

We believe in freedom of worship for all.

We believe in freedom of commerce for all.

And we believe in limited governments—all of them.

And because, in these times, what happens in one country quickly impacts others, we believe that all peoples should live free from tyranny and oppression, whether it takes the form of political oppression, economic slavery, or religious fanaticism. That fundamental idea must not remain mere words; it must be supported in deeds—diplomatically, economically, and materially—through the combined strength of all countries that stand for freedom.

This doctrine of the new Argentina is no more and no less than the true essence of the United Nations Organization: the cooperation of the United Nations in defense of freedom. If the United Nations decides to return to the principles that gave it life and to once again adopt the role for which it was conceived, you can count on the unwavering support of Argentina in the struggle for freedom.

You should also know that Argentina will not support any policy that implies the restriction of individual freedoms, of trade, or the violation of the natural rights of individuals, no matter who promotes it or how much consensus that institution has.

For this reason, we wish to express—officially—our dissent on the Pact for the Future, signed on Sunday, and we invite all the nations of the free world to join us, not only in dissenting from this pact but also in the creation of a new agenda for this noble institution: the agenda of freedom.

From this day on, know that the Argentine Republic will abandon the position of historical neutrality that has characterized us and will be at the forefront of the struggle in defense of freedom.

Because—as Thomas Paine said—*"those who wish to reap the blessings of freedom must, like men, undergo the fatigue of supporting it."*

May God bless the Argentines and all the citizens of the world, and may the forces of heaven be with us.

Long live freedom!

Thank you very much. (English translation via DeepL from casarosada.gob.ar as prepared for delivery of Spanish language document.)

APPENDIX 5D: PODCAST RECOMMENDATIONS

Thomas Sowell is brilliant and the most important advocate of empirical evidence validating or disproving socioeconomic theories. He is the most-quoted individual in our quote appendix. The following podcast demonstrates this and is a must-reference resource if you care about the topics presented in this book. It is The Hoover Institution's Uncommon Knowledge podcast, and the episode title is "Thomas Sowell: Facts Against Rhetoric, Capitalism—and, Yes the Tariffs."

Additionally, Curt Weldon's (past congressman) interview by Tucker Carlson titled "It Is Finally Time to Tell the Truth about 9-11" was also fascinating, and the issues he points out demonstrate the need to get rid of the Deep State for the entire world's benefit.

The intelligence, wisdom, vision, and perception of Shyam Sankar (chief technology officer of Palantir Technologies Inc.) are almost unmatched. You will find a riveting interview with him on the application of technology to warfare in "The Shawn Ryan Show" podcast number 190. We highly recommend you access it to find out what needs to be done to protect our freedoms.

And finally, Tucker Carlson had a wonderful podcast on April 23, 2025 where he interviewed George Friedman, the principal at Geopolitical Futures. Friedman gave a fascinating long-term outlook with great historical perspective talking about cyclical historical resets.

APPENDIX 6A: MEASURING VISION—TRUE NORTH, QUANTUM LEAP LOGIC, AND REVERSE ANALYSIS

Vision is often referred to without a discussion of what it actually is. It is our belief that the term represents the ability of the human to be able to see the expected results of proposed ideas in the future. This could also be referred to as human quantum leap logic.

One of our coauthors has come up with a way to measure vision quantitatively, thus allowing it to be considered when identifying and selecting individuals for offices of responsibility or to participate in certain group activities.

First, to understand vision, let's use a compass rose with vector analysis to examine the potential impact of various vision skills—or the lack thereof. Let's label the 360-degree vector as "True North." This represents the purely positive vector of organizational decision-making, reflecting pure progress. "True South" is the purely negative vector, indicating pure regression. East and West (90 and 270 degrees) are mere noise—all work and no progress.

The objective of decision-making is to be as efficient and positive as possible. **True North**, therefore, is the purest example of the best decision-making. While True North isn't easily attainable, the goal is to get as close to it in results as possible.

To move in a specific direction, one must have a "vision" of what that optimal direction is—and a defined path for how to proceed

Quantum Leap Logic is the ability to look at a situation and propose a solution at the end of a decision tree without first examining all the contributing components. This approach is used to avoid getting lost in the maze of possible paths. To test the efficiency of that solution, analyzing the path backward—from the envisioned solution to the current starting point—is an important validating exercise we call **reverse analysis**.

Therefore, vision represents the melding of creativity and quantum leap logic—the ability, in some regards, to see into the future. Knowing the desired endpoint and using reverse analysis to accurately define an efficient path is a sound application of good vision.

I was once challenged with the question, "Can you measure vision?"

Having pondered that question for quite a while, I believe I came up with a way to, in fact, "measure vision." The following provides details for fulfilling that process.

As an organizational policy, ideas need to be distributed down several separate channels. That way, the idea is "made public" and becomes known to multiple people who do not share the same channel. This enhances the probability of the author receiving due recognition and prevents theft of the idea. The system can become part of each individual's "report card" on their skill set.

Steps to Measure Vision

1. The corporation or organization puts in place an idea database.

2. Any individual may supply a written idea which is submitted to the database and receives a time stamp. The individual then must forward the database submission to a minimum of two individuals in separate channels:

    a. To immediate boss (out of historical respect for the hierarchy) in the author's current department structure is required; and

b. Another individual or individuals (of the author's choice) outside the author's current historical channel

3. The individuals receiving the idea have three potential responses

    a. "+" positive reflection—the idea has potential for making a positive contribution

    b. "-" negative reflection—the idea doesn't offer much potential or is expected to fail

    c. "0"—this neutral response creates a neutral product (zero times any number yields zero; effectively there is no opinion being voiced)

4. Any individual in the organization may put their response on any database submissions before a deadline date.

5. Organizational decisions to move ahead with further investigation can lead to a quantitative number showing stage progress.

6. Beta stage testing—lower loss exposure for risk purposes in analyzing the idea's potential.

    a. Positive or negative results in the quantitative form are multiplied by the individual's response.

    b. If the idea has a positive outcome and the individual responds with a "+," the individual gets a positive product added to their "vision recognition" record.

c. If the idea has a positive outcome and the individual responds with a "-," then that individual would receive a negative product for their "vision recognition" record.

d. If the idea has a negative outcome, then the positive respondent would get a negative product due to their "+" response.

e. If the idea has a negative outcome, then the negative respondent would get a positive product due to their "-" response.

7. Successive stages of advance testing would yield larger products due to larger beta tests prior to final implementation.

8. Implementation—this will yield ongoing products going into the individual's "vision recognition" record.

9. Participants in testing up to and including implementation get points for effectiveness in carrying out their role:

    a. Suggesting improvements that are implemented get points in participants' "vision recognition" record

    b. Proficiency in carrying out their responsibilities results in a separate manner of recognition for making a valuable contribution in assisting to bring ideas to fruition through the testing and implementation stages

Committee investigators and project implementers get recognition also for facilitating the development and progress of "visions."

APPENDIX 6B: SUCCESSOR PLANNING

One of the greatest problems for organizations is having the next generation of managers who are true leaders be ready and in a position to take on the mantle of responsibility when the current officeholder is set to depart.

What do you think is the most important activity in a ten- to twenty-year period that the board of directors (BOD) has? Isn't it selecting a successor CEO? A great decision not only benefits the organization but also makes the BOD's job much easier in its supervisory oversight role. Finding an exemplary leader (fulfilling our definition of leadership) who also possesses vision skills is the ultimate "corporate/organizational find."

To show how important this is, look no further than the following:

1. Tesla—Elon Musk
2. Amazon—Jeff Bezos
3. Microsoft—Satya Nadella
4. Apple—Steve Jobs
5. Southwest Airlines—Herb Kelleher
6. General Electric—Jack Welch

Conversely, look at other CEOs from some of those companies, and you will see several examples of how badly things can go wrong. Some CEOs were the original founders, demonstrating amazing vision. Others may have had success, but their successors did not always fare as well. It seems that successor planning is not widely done well. In fact, some CEOs purposefully try to ensure there are no high-caliber potential replacements in place so that the organization remains dependent on them.

Therefore, considering some of the examples above—both successful and mediocre—wouldn't it be useful to have a method to measure corporate vision? The success and sustainability of an organization may well depend on having a visionary leader in place. This then begs the question: Are we subject to the board of directors' (BODs') "gut feelings"? Or wouldn't we be better off if we could provide a method for BODs to have statistical information that would yield a strong indication of various candidates' vision skills?

The rhetorical question is this: Can you "measure vision"? Many have said no when asked that question. Now, with your Critical Thinking skills being developed, determine if the following might be not only helpful but also a consistent way to analyze senior management candidates—up to and including CEO candidates.

Within an organization, there are several different departments. Historically, subordinates have given their ideas to their bosses. While that was acceptable in the past, that singular process is fraught with potential conflicts beyond simple acceptance:

1. The boss may treat the idea as their own immediately.

2. The boss may file the idea away so that they can "surface" it later and take credit. (*This happened to one of this book's authors. The solution was handled politically within the department's hierarchy.*)

3. The boss may simply turn down the idea.

4. The boss may have the idea presented to an internal department committee, where it may be dismissed for "political purposes"

since individuals may see the creator as a political rival, competing for recognition and advancement.

Every successful organization with normal longevity will require successive CEOs or managing directors. Should the board of directors leave the process to intuition, or shouldn't they have a more formal and rigorous system? One idea for such a system is to build succession into the very structure under which the organization operates.

Taking a typical organization, the dominant departments are the following:

1. Operations—COO (chief operating officer)
2. Finance—CFO (chief financial officer)
3. Marketing—CMO (chief marketing officer)
4. Technology and Technological Security—CTO (chief technology officer) (*possibly another key department*)

Human resources, while an important department, is not typically considered a pipeline for selecting the next CEO.

To turn this thought process on its head, consider that the three chief officers listed above and possibly the CTO, who are the typical candidates from which an internal CEO might be selected. However, to improve the succession process, let's investigate some considerations further.

If a succession plan is to be improved, shouldn't we reduce the role of intuition?

Therefore, if human resources is the repository for all employment information and is used extensively for promotion decisions, couldn't it also be used for the apex of career aspirations?

As a result, we suggest that the process of CEO succession take the form of selecting the next CEO while they are still the executive vice president (EVP) for human resources—where all employee data resides.

This way, the CEO's right-hand person focuses on employees, identifying those with the most potential across all departments and placing them on a fast track for development. In doing so, the EVP for human resources would likely be selected from the EVPs of operations, finance, or marketing.

This individual then serves as the CEO's right-hand person while simultaneously being the automatic heir apparent. When the CEO departs, the EVP for human resources assumes the CEO position, and the next EVP for human resources is selected by the BOD.

APPENDIX 6C: CYCLE OF FREEDOM

In trying to develop this body of work to help individuals understand the requirements, areas of intellectual contribution, structures of government, and economic systems in which we all function, it helps to understand cycles in society. Alexander Tytler supplies an interesting theory that assists in analyzing where society is in those cycles at any point in time.

The following article "Cycle of Freedom" is by Jeff Thomas:

> Periodically, I offer up a statement by Scottish economist Alexander Tytler, who, in 1787, was reported to have commented on the then-new American Republic as follows:
>
> A democracy is always temporary in nature; it simply cannot exist as a permanent form of government. A democracy will continue to exist up until the time that voters discover they can vote themselves generous gifts from the public treasury. From that moment on, the majority always votes for the candidates who promise the most benefits from the public treasury, with the result that every democracy will finally collapse due to loose fiscal policy, which is always followed by a dictatorship.
>
> The average age of the world's greatest civilizations has been about 200 years. These nations always progressed through this sequence:
>
> From Bondage to Moral Certitude;

from Moral Certitude to Great Courage;

from Great Courage to Liberty;

from Liberty to Abundance;

from Abundance to Selfishness;

from Selfishness to Complacency;

from Complacency to Apathy;

from Apathy to Dependency;

from Dependency to Bondage.

Tytler had it right. There is a *Freedom Cycle*. It's not an accident. It's based upon human nature, which is perennial. And it's not something that can be manipulated to suddenly reverse itself, just because the citizens of a country are unhappy when they find themselves living in the declining stages. *It has to play itself out.*

Tytler was quite a scholar and had come to his conclusion, based upon the rise and fall of *many* nations, over the ages, with particular emphasis on the Athenian Republic.

Since Tytler's time, we've been able to witness many formerly free countries slide inexorably into their final stages of decline.

For example, the countries in the EU are further gone than the countries in North America, and Venezuela is further gone, still.

But, what this means is that the cycle is likely to stay in order in these countries over time and, at some point, years from now, Venezuela will be likely to climb out of its Bondage stage before Europe and certainly before North America.

What very few people can wrap their heads around, is that this is indeed a *cycle. And* cycles *never* reverse themselves.

The Freedom Cycle continues until it hits bottom (Bondage), then it *stays* there for a while. Historically, the generation that is in charge at the time of bondage is *never* responsible for the eventual rebirth. The bottom must continue long enough for a new generation of adults (who, all their lives have witnessed that "free stuff" is a lie) to create the rebirth. They understand, only too well, that their only hope to have more, is to develop a work ethic and stick to it. (Their still-whining parents continue to hope that a leader will come along and finally deliver the free lunch.)

The cycle is a long one, as it requires that generations pass. Just as the depression-era people in the US and Europe were hard working and the baby boomers were their spoiled children who voted for those who promised free stuff, and millennials represent the complacency and apathy generation, so these generations must age and slide into the background before a new and productive generation can create a rebirth.

I was extraordinarily fortunate. In my own country, when I was young, we were relatively poor but hardworking people who understood that if we didn't work, we didn't eat. We didn't get to build houses for ourselves and we didn't buy a car. Therefore, everyone except the truly indigent worked. The *truly* indigent are always very few in any culture, and our entire community looked after them easily, without government support.

But, then came dramatic prosperity. One of the by-products of that prosperity was that a new generation of politicians rose up, hoping to cash in. They promised free stuff to the public but insisted that they must be left alone to dominate. (Their dual slogans were, "The people may have their say, but Government must have its way," and, "We were elected to govern and govern, we shall.")

But small numbers of us challenged them, dug in our heels, and, over time, we gained overwhelming support from our people. We had to rout two successive governments, but, eventually, those political hopefuls who remained, understood that, should they become too domineering, their careers would end. As Thomas Jefferson said, "When government fears the people, there is liberty. When the people fear the government, there is tyranny."

In Jefferson's day, America had been a frontier. Those who went there to find freedom from the oppression in Europe understood that, if they were to survive there, they must have a strong work ethic and be entirely self-reliant. They were soon joined by others from Europe with a similar ethic.

These were not people who would tolerate dominance. Although the colonists only paid King George a meager 2% in tax, they revolted at the very principle of domination and, through their tenacity, prevailed. (Remember, the *majority* of them were self-reliant.)

The same was true in my own country. People who have a strong work ethic and are self-reliant may be kind and sharing, but they don't like being dictated to. Therefore, when we opposed the tyranny that had just begun in our country, we attracted tremendous support from the electorate. (Again, the *majority* were self-reliant.)

Cuba, today is just breaking out of the ground in its own rebirth. Although it is not yet understood by most of the world, a younger generation of free marketers has grown to adulthood in a country where the "free stuff" has been an obvious lie. Their parents remain complacent and apathetic, whilst the new generation are transforming their country *from the bottom up* and their trajectory is unstoppable.

If there is a lesson to be learned here, it is that a Freedom Cycle exists and has always existed and it's driven by human nature. Most people, when they find themselves in the downward swing of the cycle, become complacent and apathetic, as Tytler describes. Otherwise intelligent, educated people vainly hope for a Freedom Fairy who will appear on the scene and reverse the process (but will continue giving out the free stuff).

Historically, this has *never* happened. No country reverses the cycle. Like a plant, it must die before renewal can occur. So, the reader may wish to ponder where his own country is on Tytler's list of stages. If it's on the upward swing, wonderful—life will be good until it reaches the pivot point of "Abundance to Selfishness." (From "Doug Casey's International Man," February 3, 2025)

ACKNOWLEDGMENTS

I want to thank my wife for her 24/7 support throughout this multi-year project. She truly is the personification of critical thinking and provided invaluable insight, suggestions, critique, and encouragement as I sought to become a published author! She is truly my everything.

I too want to thank the consistent, focused, compassionate interest in our efforts from the StoryBuilders team, who worked diligently over the months to professionally nudge and encourage us towards clarity and readability of what could have been a dry tome of academic structure, but which has in our judgment become a living documentation of what is good and great within the United States, and how to preserve what we cherish for ourselves, our families, our society, and our future. This thank you applies specifically to Bill Blankschaen and Jen Truitt, dedicated members of the StoryBuilders team.

I also want to thank the management of The Quail Valley River and Golf Club for the hospitality and gracious support of our hundred-plus lunches as we met to review and write our book. Our model pamphlet was "Common Sense" by Thomas Paine. As often as we reached impasse, and rabbit trails of thought and intent, we came always back to the model and guiding principles of common sense as identified in "Common Sense." Kevin Given and the entire staff (including Kenny, Samantha, Cassandra, and the many dedicated members of the staff of the River Club)—Thank you!

Further encouragement came from countless friends across the country over the several years. It took time for the concept of Critical Thinking to bore into the brains of some of our friends, but in the end they all began to appreciate the reasons for our writing, and the reasons for why we cared and care so much about our country and its future. They all know who they are. Thank you.

Peter H. Calfee

Without my dedicated and understanding wife I could never have gotten to where I am today. She has seen me through the good and the bad. She has overlooked the flaws and forgiven. She has allowed me to go off on my mental adventures in search of the truth. She is my Rock. Also, my mother Phyllis was dedicated to my understanding of things and is responsible for any of the good attributes I may possess. We have gone through three deep edits. The first was by my gifted daughter, Wallis. She did her incredible work out of love to give something back to her father. I will be forever grateful. James Hallman did the second deep edit and added a wonderful perspective further refining our message. And the final edit and preparation for publishing was performed by the wonderful team at StoryBuilders. In particular, I would like to thank Bill Blankschaen and Jen Truitt from that team for their incredible work and patience with us.

Additionally and finally, I would like to thank Kevin Given and his team at the Quail Valley Club, which created the optimal environment for Peter's and my collaborative luncheon meetings. Special thanks to Samantha and Kenny.

J. Kevin Dolan

ABOUT THE AUTHORS

PETER H. CALFEE

Peter earned his B.A. from Stanford University and his M.B.A. from the University of Chicago. He is a retired CPA, CFP®, and CLU. Peter was honorably discharged as a First Lieutenant in the United States Army Reserves and has served as an Adjunct Professor at several institutions, including Hiram College, Lake Erie College, and in the Financial Planning programs at John Carroll University and Myers University.

Over the course of his career, Peter has held significant leadership roles in both professional and nonprofit organizations. He served as Chair of the CFP Board of Examiners and was a member of the CFP Board of Governors, bringing with him extensive experience in SEC and FINRA regulatory matters.

Peter has also contributed his financial expertise to numerous nonprofit and community boards. These include serving as Treasurer and Board Member of The Cleveland Museum of Natural History, Treasurer of Bent Pine Country Club and the Community Church of Vero Beach, and Treasurer and Finance/Investment Committee Chair of the United Way Foundation of Indian River. His HOA leadership includes roles as Treasurer and Board Member at the River Club at

Carleton, Champion Lane/Ohio HOA, and Bonnie Briar Circle HOA in Charlotte, North Carolina. He also served on the Board of the Judson Retirement Community in Cleveland and Chagrin Falls, Ohio, and currently sits on the advisory board of the Florida Highway Patrol.

Peter and his wife, Jan, reside in Vero Beach, Florida, and maintain a townhouse in Charlotte, North Carolina. Their two grown sons, both of whom work in the finance industry, live in Charlotte with their wives and five children.

J. KEVIN DOLAN

Kevin earned his B.A. in Economics from Denison University in 1973. After completing pilot training in the U.S. Air Force, he flew C-141s on active duty as well as in the Air Force Reserves. Kevin was hired by American Airlines at the end of 1977 and concurrently earned his M.B.A. from The Wharton School in 1981 and his CFP® designation in 1987.

While at American, Kevin led the union's (The Allied Pilots Association) due diligence efforts to establish a credit union. The Allied Pilots Federal Credit Union began operations in January 1994 and was quickly recognized as an early adopter of electronic banking services. Kevin served on its Board of Directors from its inception.

Kevin retired as a pilot in 2010 but remained actively involved with the pilot community, leveraging his business expertise.

He was an early member and eventual partner in the Lifetime Asset Management Program (LAMP), a Registered Investment Advisory (RIA) firm. LAMP provided asset management services to pilots approaching retirement. Kevin developed the key equation used in the firm's "Final Approach" marketing program, which helped pilots optimize their retirement timing decisions.

LAMP later merged with Pritchard and Herr Associates to become Pritchard, Hubble & Herr. The firm subsequently acquired Retirement Advisors of America (RAA) and continued operations under that name until it was acquired by Allworth Financial. During his tenure with these firms, Kevin served as East Coast Director, designed the Investment Policy Statement for clients, revised an early version of the annual Retirement Resource Review (a comprehensive financial check-up for clients), and held roles as Strategic Planning Director, CFO, and Board Member. RAA, now known as Allworth Airline Advisors, was acquired by Allworth Financial after Kevin's retirement.

Kevin and his wife, Marcia, reside in Vero Beach, Florida, where they greatly enjoy their activities at the Quail Valley Club.

To connect with Peter and Kevin, please visit HijackedOurRepublic.com

INDEX

Accountability – 5, 20, 21, 43, 112, 114, 130
Action steps (personal / civic) – 112, 113, 129
Adaptability / Progress – 103, 104
Alinsky, Saul – 23, 24, 25, 123–125
America / American values – 3, 4, 5, 8, 11, 29, 33, 43, 49, 111–114, 117, 129
Anarchy – 24
Ancient deities (e.g., Baal, Ra, Zeus, Mars) – 45
Appendices (referenced) – 11, 17, 19, 21, 31, 38, 41, 110
Aristotle – 31
Articles of Confederation – 49
Arts, the – 35, 36
Authoritarianism / Radical activism – 4, 123–125
Ayatollah (Iran) – 3
Bastiat, Frederic – 20
Belief systems / Worldviews – 45–47
Bill of Rights – 29, 49, 141
Bin Laden, Osama – 24
Bolsheviks – 23
British Empire – 2
Bureaucracy / Bureaucracies – 38, 39, 40

Bush, George W. – 40
Capitalism / Free-market economy – 91–96, 100
Causality – 18, 19, 28, 63
Censorship – 27
Character traits (ideal) – 28, 29, 109
Charter schools – 41
Chavez, Hugo – 3
Checks and balances – 72, 73, 84
Cicero – 48
Citizenship / Civic duty – 84, 126–130
Class warfare – 26, 79
Common sense – 17, 18, 34, 48, 63, 104
Communism – 3, 23, 24, 72, 73, 75, 77, 91, 92, 95, 96
Competition (education/economy/leadership) – 38, 40, 41, 92–94, 100, 104, 106
Constitution, U.S. – 1, 3, 15, 21, 29, 49, 92, 104, 105, 109, 138–145
Constitutional Convention – 140
Constitutional republic – 72, 73, 74
Critical Thinking – 1–3, 6–7, 14–31, 33–36, 38, 40, 43, 47, 49–50, 61–63, 72, 84, 91–92, 94, 103–105, 108–110, 111–113, 129, 131

Cuba / Venezuela / Nicaragua
– 3, 72, 91, 92

Dalio, Ray – 39
Debt (national / personal) – 26, 91
Declaration of Independence
– 2, 15, 49, 138–139
Democratic Republic (U.S.) – 27
Dictatorship / Totalitarianism
– 3, 22–25, 72, 75–77
Disinformation – 7
Economic classes / Mobility – 91–93
Economic literacy – 92–94
Economic Systems – 1,
10, 34, 37, 91–102
Education – 2, 3, 6–8, 10–11, 33–44,
92, 103–104, 106, 111, 126–128
Einstein, Albert – 31, 34
Empires (historical) – 2, 61
Enlightenment – 21
Entrepreneurship – 91, 93
Equality / Equal opportunity
– 42, 43, 92, 100
Eternal truths – 4–7, 9–10,
30, 61–63, 104, 110
Ethics / Moral codes / Morality –
20, 31, 34, 36–37, 45–46, 49–50,
92–93, 100, 117, 129–130
Faith / Spirituality / Judeo-Christian
values – 3, 6–8, 10, 34, 36, 45–51,
100, 104, 110, 117, 133–135
Family / Parenting – 5, 6, 33–34, 46
Federalism – 140
Founders / Founding Fathers /
Quotes – 2, 15, 21, 27, 72–74,
105, 115–117, 133–135

Freedom (speech, religion,
thought) – 3, 17, 20–22, 27, 46,
49, 62–63, 72–75, 91–94, 100,
104–106, 133–135, 138–141
Future generations – 9, 11,
43, 103–104, 113
Golden Rule – 49
Goebbels, Joseph – 23
Government (structure, trust,
transparency) – 3, 15, 22–23, 38,
72–77, 104–106, 112–114, 140
Greed / Self-interest – 5, 93
Gutenberg Bible – 37
Health care policy – 25
History – 1–4, 6–10, 14–15, 19,
21, 23, 34–36, 39, 41, 43, 46,
61–70, 104–106, 126–128, 133
Hitler, Adolf – 23, 75
Home plate (metaphor) – 5
Human nature / Development
– 1, 4–5, 8–10, 61, 63
Indoctrination / Activism – 3,
21–22, 34, 38, 76–77, 123–125
Inequality – 43
Innovation – 39
Integrity (values / leadership)
– 23, 28, 104, 109
Iran (Mullahs) – 3, 24, 72
Islamic extremism / ISIS
/ Al-Qaeda – 24
Jefferson, Thomas – (contextual
references only)
Judgment (good judgment) – 17–19
Justice / Fairness – 5, 49

Kim family (North Korea) – 24, 72
Knowledge – 7–8, 34–36, 61, 63
Leadership / Civic roles / Traits – 43, 84, 106, 109, 111–114
Lenin, Vladimir – 21, 73
Liberty / Individual rights / Natural rights – 1, 3–5, 21, 27, 73–75, 91–93, 104–105, 113, 115–117, 139–141
Logic / Logical thinking – 17–19, 35, 38
Marx, Karl / Marxism – 23, 73, 95
Maslow's hierarchy / Self-actualization – 34
Millei, Javier – 20
Mob rule / Revolutionary violence – 21
Monarchy (Russian) – 23
Moral relativism vs. absolutes – 45, 50
Moses / Mount Sinai – 46
Mussolini, Benito – 22, 23, 75
Natural law / Social contract – 19, 21, 74
North Korea – 24, 72
No Child Left Behind (policy) – 40
Ortega, Daniel – 3, 72
Paine, Thomas – 32
Parental roles / Family structure – 5–6, 33–34
Party rule / One-party systems – 3, 23, 72, 75–77
Patriotism – 27, 113, 129
Philosophy (Western) – 50
Pilgrims / Religious freedom – 49
Pol Pot – 3, 72
Political Systems – 1, 10, 19, 24, 37, 72–90, 105
Printing press – 37
Progress / Human advancement – 1, 3–5, 8–10, 34, 61–63, 103–105
Propaganda / Misinformation – 23, 76
Public schools – 41
Purpose (individual/national) – 8
Putin, Vladimir – 24, 72
Quotes (Founders / Freedom / Truth) – 115–117, 133–135
Rand, Ayn – 31
Reading / Writing / Literacy – 34–35
Reformation / Protestantism – 49
Regulation / Bureaucracy – 25–26, 38–40, 94–95
Religion / Religious teachings – 1, 3, 7–8, 10, 34, 36, 45–51, 104, 117, 133
Responsibility / Moral courage / Citizenship – 5, 20–21, 43, 91, 100, 104, 109, 111–114
Revolutions (France, Russia) – 21, 23
Rights (civil, constitutional, inalienable) – 3–5, 21, 27, 73–75, 91–93, 105, 139–141
Rome / Roman Republic – 2, 21
Rousseau, Jean-Jacques – 19
Rule of law – 20, 74, 92, 139–141
Rules for Radicals – 24–25, 123–125
School systems / Curriculum – 35–36, 40–41
Self-interest / Greed – 5, 93
Social contract – 19, 21, 74, 115, 140
Social fabric / Civil society – 2, 19–20
Socialism – 3, 23, 72–73, 75, 77, 91–92, 95–96
Socrates / Plato (implied) – 47
Spain / Portuguese empires – 2
Speech (freedom of) – 3, 17, 21, 27
Spirituality – 8, 34, 46

Stalin, Joseph – 3, 23, 73
Standards / Expectations – 5–6, 42
Supreme Court – 18, 73
Teachers / Teaching – 6, 34, 38, 40, 41
Technology / AI – 6–7, 34, 39
Terrorism / Extremism – 24
Thatcher, Margaret – 32
Thinking (free, critical) – 1–3, 6, 14–31
Toynbee, Arnold – 29
Transparency (elections / government) – 22, 73, 84
Truth / Eternal truth – 4–7, 10, 30, 61–63, 104, 110, 115–117, 131, 133–135
United States (U.S.) – 1–5, 10, 15, 27, 29, 38, 49, 72–75, 91–94, 100, 104–106
Values / Value systems – 1–3, 6, 8, 10, 17, 27, 34, 36–37, 45–51, 92–93, 100, 104–106, 110
Violence / Force / Power grabs – 4, 22–23
Virtue / Civic virtue – 31–32, 49, 133–135
Voltaire – 31
Voting / Elections – 22, 73, 84, 113, 126–130
War (historical, ideological) – 46
Washington, George (quoted) – 133
Western civilization / Western man – 50
Wisdom / Reason – 17–19, 131–132
Work ethic / Labor – 37
World Economic Forum (Millei speech) – 20
Writing / Communication – 34–35

Chapter 1: Critical Thinking

Alinsky, Saul – 24, 25
Anarchy – 24
Appendices (referenced) – 17, 19, 21, 31
Bastiat, Frederic – 20
Bin Laden, Osama – 24
Black Brigade (Mussolini) – 22
Causality – 18, 19
Character traits (ideal) – 28, 29
Common sense – 17, 18
Communism – 3 (referenced again in ch. 1, p. 23)
Critical Thinking – 14–31 (core focus throughout)
Democratic Republic (U.S.) – 27
Dictatorship / Totalitarianism – 22–25
Einstein, Albert – 31
Eternal truths – 10, 30
Fascism – 23
Freedom (thought, questioning, speech) – 17, 21, 22, 27
Goebbels, Joseph – 23
Hitler, Adolf – 23
Indoctrination – 21, 22
Judgment – 18, 19
Kim family (North Korea) – 24
Logic / Logical reasoning – 17–19
Millei, Javier – 20
Mussolini, Benito – 22, 23
Natural rights / Natural law – 21
Pol Pot – 3 (again referenced in ch. 1)
Political fabric / Social fabric – 19, 20
Premise / Argument structure – 19
Questions / Questioning – 14, 17, 18, 21
Rand, Ayn – 31
Rights (inalienable) – 21
Rousseau, Jean-Jacques (social contract) – 19
Rules for Radicals – 24, 25
Saul Alinsky (see Alinsky, Saul) –
Stalin, Joseph – 3 (referred to again here in totalitarian context)
Supreme Court – 18
Terrorism / Extremism – 24
Thatcher, Margaret – 32
Toynbee, Arnold – 29
Transparency (elections) – 22
Truth / Searching for truth – 14, 30
Voltaire – 31
Wisdom – 17, 18, 19

Chapter 2: Education

Accountability – 34, 37
Albert Einstein – 34
Arts, the – 35, 36
Bureaucracy / Bureaucracies – 38, 39, 40
Carneiro, Robert – 35
Charter schools – 41
Children / Future generations – 33, 39, 43
Common sense – 34
Competition (educational) – 38, 40, 41
Creativity – 38, 39
Critical Thinking – 33, 34, 36, 38, 40, 43
Cultural literacy – 37
Curiosity – 38, 40
Dalio, Ray – 39
Discipline – 33

Educational goals / Objectives – 36, 37
Education (core focus) – 33–44
Equality / Equal opportunity – 42, 43
Esteem (Maslow) – 34
Ethics / Morality – 34, 36, 37
Faith (religious/spiritual) – 34, 36
Family unit – 34
Financial services – 37
Gutenberg Bible – 37
History (subject) – 35, 36
Homeschooling – 42
Incentives / Motivation – 34, 40
Innovation – 39
Knowledge – 34, 35, 36
Leadership (traits, selection) – 43
Learning / Rote learning – 34, 38, 40
Maslow's hierarchy – 34
Medical services – 37
Merit / Achievement – 38, 43
Parochial schools – 42
Persistence – 29 (relevant in this chapter through cross-reference)
Private schools – 41
Public schools – 41
Reading / Writing / Literacy – 35
Religion – 34, 36
Rote memorization – 34, 38, 40
Scott Looney – 41
Self-actualization – 34
Social responsibility – 39
STEAM – 38
Teaching / Teachers – 38, 40, 41
Technology / AI – 34, 39
Values / Value systems – 34, 36, 37
William Arthur Ward – 43
Work ethic / Habits – 37

Chapter 3: Religion, Faith, and Values

Allegory of the Cave (Plato) – 47
American Revolution – 49
Ancient deities (e.g., Baal, Ra, Zeus, Mars) – 45
Articles of Confederation – 49
Belief systems / Worldviews – 45–47
Christianity / Christ – 48
Cicero – 48
Civilizations / Cultural values – 46, 48, 49
Clarity of purpose – 50
Common sense – 48
Community / Social cohesion – 49
Conflict (religious/cultural) – 45, 47
Critical Thinking – 47, 49, 50
Declaration of Independence – 49
Divine judgment / Salvation – 47, 48
Ethics / Moral codes – 45, 46, 49
Faith (core theme) – 45–51
Family unit – 34, 46
Golden Rule / Reciprocity – 49
God / Divine being – 46, 47, 48, 50
Great Awakenings (U.S.) – 49
Guidance / Moral foundation – 45, 46, 50
Historical teachings – 46, 47
Idolatry / Golden calf (Moses) – 46
Individual freedom of religion – 47, 49
Israelites / Mount Sinai (Moses) – 46
Judeo-Christian values – 50, 51
Justice / Fairness – 5, 49
Love / Respect (as religious values) – 45, 49
Moral relativism vs. absolutes – 45, 50

Moses – 46
Nature worship / Pagan religions – 45, 46
Paradise / Afterlife – 47
Pilgrims (1620) – 49
Political authority from religion – 45
Protestant Reformation – 49
Purpose of religion – 46, 48
Rationalizing human experience – 45, 48
Reciprocity (Golden Rule) – 49
Religious freedom – 47, 49
Religious misapplication / Abuse – 45, 47
Salvation – 47, 48
Self-centeredness vs. community – 49
Spirituality – 46
Ten Judeo-Christian values (Prager) – 50
Universal yearning for belief – 45, 46
Values / Value systems – 45–51
Western civilization – 50
Zeus, Ra, Mars (see Ancient deities) – 45

Chapter 4: History

Accountability (historical reflection) – 61, 63
Causality (in historical study) – 63
Civilizations (past and present) – 61, 62, 63
Common sense – 63
Community / National identity – 61
Constitution, U.S. – 63
Critical Thinking – 61–63
Cultural memory / Preservation – 63
Empires (Greek, Roman, British, etc.) – 2, 61
Ethics / Eternal truths – 61, 62, 63
Experience (learning from the past) – 61–63
Failures / Historical mistakes – 3, 62, 63
Family to nation-state evolution – 8, 61
Founding Fathers – 2, 15, 63
Freedom / Democratic values – 62, 63
Growth of humankind – 61–63
Historical analysis – 61–63
Historical data / Memory – 62, 63
Historical figures / Founders – 61, 63
Historical patterns – 63
Historical perspective / Lessons – 61–63
Human nature / Development – 61, 63
Indoctrination (vs. historical learning) – 63
Inspiration / Historical examples – 36, 62
Knowledge from history – 61, 63
Learning from the past – 61–63
Mistakes / Repetition of history – 62, 63
National evolution (historical lens) – 61
Objective learning vs. erasure – 63
Past-present-future connection – 61, 62
Political and Economic Systems – 8, 61
Preserving history (not erasing) – 63
Progress (human and societal) – 61, 62
Reflection on history – 61
Societal change through time – 61, 63
Societal development – 61, 63
Storytelling / Historical narrative – 61

Truth-seeking (through history) – 61, 63
United States (historical lens) – 2, 61, 63
Values / Eternal truths – 61–63
Witness of human growth – 61

Chapter 5: Political Systems

Accountability (in governance) – 72, 84
Alinsky, Saul – 24, 72
Authoritarianism / Autocracy – 72, 76, 77
Biden, Joe (referenced generically as current president) – 76
Checks and balances – 72, 73, 84
China / Communist Party – 72, 75
Citizenship / Civic duty – 84
Class warfare – 26, 79
Communism – 3, 72, 73, 75, 77
Constitutional republic – 72, 73, 74
Critical Thinking – 72, 84
Cuba (Castro) – 3, 72
Dictatorship / Centralized power – 3, 23, 72, 75–77
Economic Systems (interaction) – 37, 72
Elections / Transparency – 22, 73, 84
Equal protection – 74
Fascism – 3, 72, 73
Federalism – 73
Founding Fathers – 72–74
Freedom / Liberty – 72, 73, 75, 77
Government (types of) – 72–77
Hitler, Adolf – 23, 75
Human dignity / Individual rights – 74, 77

Ideological control / Indoctrination – 76, 77
Iran / Mullahs – 3, 24, 72
Kim family (North Korea) – 24, 72
Leadership / Public service – 84
Legislative process / Lawmaking – 73, 84
Lenin, Vladimir – 21, 73
Liberty / Self-governance – 73, 74
Marx, Karl / Marxism – 23, 73
Millei, Javier – 20
Mussolini, Benito – 22, 23, 75
Natural law / Rights – 21, 74
North Korea – 24, 72
One-party rule / Central control – 3, 72, 75–77
Ortega, Daniel (Nicaragua) – 3, 72
Participation in government – 84
Perón, Juan (Argentina) – 3, 72
Personal responsibility (citizens) – 72, 84
Pol Pot (Cambodia) – 3, 72
Political polarization – 76
Populism / Charismatic leadership – 76
Power concentration / Corruption – 72, 75–77
Presidency / Executive branch – 73, 76
Propaganda / Misinformation – 23, 76
Putin, Vladimir – 24, 72
Republicanism – 72, 73
Rights / Civil liberties – 73–75
Rule of law – 20, 74
Social contract – 19, 21, 74
Socialism – 3, 72, 73, 75, 77
Stalin, Joseph – 3, 23, 73
Supreme Court / Judiciary – 18, 73
Totalitarian regimes – 3, 72, 75–77

Transparency / Government trust – 22, 73
United States (system of government) – 72–75
Values / Moral foundation – 74
Venezuela / Chavez, Maduro – 3, 72
Western political thought – 50, 73

Chapter 6: Economic Systems

Accountability (in economic behavior) – 91, 93
Accumulation of wealth / Incentives – 91–93
Agrarian economy / Farming – 91
Banking / Credit systems – 93
Capitalism / Free-market economy – 91, 92, 93, 94, 95, 100
Charitable giving / Tithing – 100
Citizenship (economic role) – 92, 94
Communism (vs. capitalism) – 91, 92, 95, 96
Competition (economic) – 92–94, 100
Constitutional foundation – 92
Critical Thinking – 91, 92, 94
Cuba / Venezuela – 91, 92
Debt (individual and national) – 26, 91
Economic classes / Mobility – 91–93
Economic incentives / Motivation – 92, 93
Economic literacy / Understanding systems – 92–94
Economic Systems (core focus) – 91–102
Education and economics – 92
Entrepreneurship – 91, 93
Equality of opportunity – 92, 100

Ethics / Economic behavior – 92, 93, 100
Europe (economic models) – 95
Faith and economic values – 100
Free market – 92–94, 95, 96
Freedom / Individual responsibility – 91–94, 100
Global competition – 93, 94
Government regulation / Overreach – 25, 94, 95
Greed / Self-interest – 5, 93
Individual choice / Ownership – 91, 92
Inflation / Cost of living – 91
Labor and productivity – 91, 92
Liberty / Economic freedom – 91, 92, 93
Marx, Karl – 23, 95
Moral responsibility (economic) – 100
Poverty – 25, 91, 92
Private property – 91, 92, 95
Productivity / Efficiency – 92, 93
Public-private partnership – 94
Redistribution of wealth – 95, 96
Responsibility (economic citizenship) – 91, 100
Rights (economic freedoms) – 91–93
Rule of law (economic systems) – 92
Self-discipline / Work ethic – 91, 93
Socialism (vs. capitalism) – 3, 91, 92, 95, 96
Taxation – 92, 94
Tithing / Charitable giving – 100
United States (economic model) – 91–94, 100
Values / Economics and morality – 92, 93, 100
Venezuela – 3, 91, 92

Wealth creation / Investment – 91–93
Workforce / Economic participation – 91, 92

Concluding Thoughts

Accountability (societal and personal) – 104, 106
Action steps / Civic engagement – 104, 109
Adaptability / Progress – 103, 104
Appendices (referenced) – 110
Awareness / Public consciousness – 103, 105
Character traits (ideal) – 28 (referenced again in tone on 109)
Common sense – 104
Competition (ideas / leadership) – 104, 106
Constitution / Founding principles – 104, 105, 109
Critical Thinking – 103–105, 108–110
Cultural division / Polarization – 104
Decision-making – 104, 105
Education (importance of) – 103, 104, 106
Eternal truths – 104, 110
Faith / Religious values – 104, 110
Founding Fathers – 105
Freedom / Individual liberty – 104–106
Future generations – 103, 104
Government accountability / Public service – 104–106
History (lessons from) – 104–106
Ideological threats – 105
Individual vs. collective – 103, 105
Integrity / Public morality – 104, 109
Leadership / Civic roles – 106, 109
Liberty / Constitutional values – 104, 105
Moral courage / Responsibility – 104, 109
Nation-building / Societal renewal – 103, 106
Natural rights / Inalienable freedoms – 105
Optimism / Hope – 103, 104
Political Systems (reviewed briefly) – 105
Progress / Societal change – 103–105
Public discourse / Dialogue – 104, 106
Religious freedom / Faith and governance – 104
Social contract (implied) – 105
Teamwork / Unity – 104, 109
Truth / Search for meaning – 104, 110
Values / Shared morality – 104–106, 110
Vision / Future direction – 103–105, 110

Appendices

Accountability – 112, 114, 130
Action steps (personal / civic) – 112, 113, 129
Alinsky, Saul (Rules for Radicals) – 123–125
American values / Founding principles – 111–114, 117, 129
Appendix A (What Can I Do?) – 111–114

Appendix B (Quotes to Consider) – 115–117
Appendix C (Rules for Radicals Excerpt) – 123–125
Appendix D (Civics Literacy Quiz) – 126–128
Appendix E (American Mind Quiz) – 129–130
Appendix F (To Think About) – 131–132
Appendix G (Founders' Quotes) – 133–135
Appendix H (Authors' Backgrounds) – 136–137
Appendix I (Constitution / Declaration excerpts) – 138–145
Authoritarianism / Radical activism – 123–125
Bill of Rights (quoted) – 141
Civics knowledge / Civic duty – 126–130
Constitution, U.S. (excerpts) – 138–145
Constitutional Convention – 140
Critical Thinking – 111–113, 129, 131
Declaration of Independence (excerpts) – 138–139
Democracy / Republic – 113, 140
Dissent / Civil discourse – 111, 113
Education / Literacy – 111, 126–128
Elections / Government transparency – 129
Ethics / Morality – 117, 129, 130
Faith / Religious principles – 117, 133–135
Federalism – 140

Founders / Founding Fathers – 115–117, 133–135
Freedom / Liberty – 112, 115–117, 133–135, 138–141
Future generations – 113
Government accountability – 112, 113, 140
Historical literacy – 126–128, 133
Indoctrination / Activist strategies – 123–125
Individual responsibility – 111–114, 130
Judeo-Christian values – 117, 133
Leadership / Civic engagement – 111–114
Liberty / Natural rights – 113, 115–117, 139–141
Morality / Moral courage – 115–117, 129–130
Natural rights / Human dignity – 115–117, 139–141
Patriotism – 113, 129
Quotes (Founders / Freedom / Truth) – 115–117, 133–135
Radicalization / Rules for Radicals – 123–125
Reflection / Self-assessment – 131–132
Rule of law – 139–141
Self-governance – 111–114, 140
Social contract – 115, 140
Truth / Enlightenment ideals – 115–117, 131, 133–135
Virtue / Civic virtue – 133–135
Voting / Citizenship – 113, 126–130
Washington, George (quoted) – 133
Wisdom / Reason – 131–132

www.ingramcontent.com/pod-product-compliance
Lightning Source LLC
Chambersburg PA
CBHW060947050426
42337CB00052B/1621